Acknowledgements

Bur Oak Chronicles is based on facts known about bur oak tree growth. Bur oaks and oaks in general are monecious, meaning 1 house. They have male and female flowers on the same tree. Therefore, in this tale, a male or female voice may represent the tree.

Many Thanks!!

To Dr. Bill Chaney, whose 1993 Tree Physiology course at Purdue University's Department of Forestry and Natural Resources, sparked the idea while I was preparing an assignment on bur oak trees. Yes, I have been working on it since then.

To my Nurnberg American High School classmates who've encouraged me to finish the story and countless other friends and family who've supported me in this endeavor.

To my marvelous illustrator, Kristin Calhoun http://kristin-calhoun.squarespace.com/ who made the project beautiful and fun.

To Maura Heaphy, who gave me valuable advice about characters in the story. To my editors, Sherry Gasper of long, long ago and more recently Roseanne Rini.

Dedication

To my grandchildren

Lance, Katelyn, Simon, Annalise, and Corban.

I hope they enjoy trees and nature as much as I do!

Chapter 1 – Lost or Found?

I was lost! Jamie McPherson, star reporter, lost!! My first assignment with the *Forester Gazette* - down the tube! I could hear the Chief chuckling now: "Check out the story of the giant trees moving from place to place. Then you can report it as an urban or in this case rural myth!!" He chortled loudly! I think he was testing me to see if I'd actually go out and now, I'm lost!

I kicked the brown dust at my feet and thrashed my hat around at the powdery particles floating towards my face! Hack! Hack! This is what happens when a city reporter moves to the middle of Kansas. How am I going to finish my bur oak report? Where are my landmarks, buildings, concrete, or billboards? How can I find my way with vast expanses of nothing! Not even a simple sign post! Humph! What kind of place is this? Why did I accept this assignment? How am I supposed to find Bur Oak, Kansas? AUGH!!

I slumped against the dusty door of my trusty, yellow jeep. The sun stood over my head like an exclamation point. Salty sweat rolled into my eyes and I was hot and hungry. What better thing to do now than eat lunch and reread my editor's directions? I yanked the crumpled map off the front seat and remembered the last sign I saw said "Bur Oak – 52 miles." That was about 80 miles ago! I was sure the ranger man in the green truck I met at the sign said I was on the right path. Could he have been wrong? I grabbed my thermal lunch sack, removed my turkey on marbled rye, clutched my cold canteen of water, folded my legs beneath me and collapsed to the ground in the little shade my jeep could provide. Munching furiously, I focused on a small, grayish dust spiral to the east and noticed the puffy clouds beginning to dot the sky like a painting taking shape. You seldom see that in Chicago.. Yawning, I watched a large-winged, brown bird squeak as it floated above my head. I wondered if it might be an eagle as I watched it circle lazily, catch an updraft and hover for a heartbeat. Looking for lunch I presumed. Closing my eyes between bites, thinking of my predicament, I slouched ever closer to the ground.

Suddenly I was coughing madly. Dust and sand filled my eyes, nose, and mouth. Blech!! A brown fog covered me. Where did this come from?

Chapter 2   *Branching Out with Cork*

I jumped up to get a better look and a tree branch smacked me across my upper arm. I turned toward the offender. "Hey! Watch what you're do…?" I was staring into the face of a real, live tree!! "AUGH!!" I screamed. "AUGH!" the tree screamed back as it ran off.

Oh, my granny! I must be losing my mind, too much heat, not enough water. No, I'm not crazy. I saw it. There was an eye, two eyes squished into the bark, and a slit for a mouth that was moving and screaming! The eyes looked at me with astonishment or fear; I couldn't tell. It happened so fast! The branches or arms or whatever they were, waved and flailed all over in its haste to get away from me. I looked down at the mark on my arm to prove it to myself. This is nuts! I stumbled back against my jeep, scrambled to the hood, and realizing I was holding my breath, filled my lungs with grimy air and coughed violently. Standing on the hood, I looked for evidence of the tree and there it was, lumbering down the little hill with rumbling and scratching sounds toward a grove of trees. And dirt, everywhere a trail of dirt followed the tree.

The sound and dust died away as the tree moved further from me. Then, I heard more; it started low like your stomach rumbling just before dinner. I peered in the direction of the sound and spied more brown puffy clouds coming from the west side of the prairie. Hastily, I jumped in my jeep and headed for what my eyes couldn't believe. As I drove I saw movement and more dust clouds along all points of the compass. What was happening?

I drove toward a spot where all the trees converged, ventured as close as I dared, and parked. Quietly, I exited my jeep and walked slowly like a gymnast on a balance beam into a grove of trees that were walking with me! And they were talking! I heard voices from every direction.

"You said we're here, but where is here?" A disgruntled small tree said to a larger one. Another said, "I wanted to stay home and be with my friends!" The tree alongside it said, "And I told her, if you let those squirrels bring leaves into your tree, they'll stay all winter!"

The strangest assemblage I had ever seen was unrolling before my eyes. I twisted and turned so fast that I made myself dizzy and sick. Trees gathered together like they were having small meetings. I inched toward the closest group. I was either invisible to them or they didn't care that I was there. No one – er tree – paid any attention to me.

Two large trees were having an animated discussion with a willowy sapling hanging nearby. Its branches waved all around as if it was giving directions. I thought of my Uncle Louie and chuckled. You had to be ever watchful when he talked. Hands and arms flew like they were swatting mosquitoes on a hot summer evening.

"Once the clans arrive," I overheard "Uncle Louie" say, "join whichever group is telling the story you want to hear. Nobody wants to miss a word and the elders are so committed to passing on information, they are willing to repeat what they know to all interested listeners. But hurry, you might miss the beginning! Get to the closest group!"

The other tree nodded, grabbed the twig of the small one, and headed in the direction of a circle forming around a massive tree. I followed in wonder. Trees telling stories! A row of thin, spindly, tannish-colored trees, maybe two-three inches in diameter, sat below a towering, multi-branched tree. It was huge! I bet my eight cousins would have trouble circling his trunk with their arms spread wide. When this tree begins to talk, I suspect it could put Grandma Helen out of the talking business! She loves telling stories of her grandparents. I listened eagerly while inching my way through the stems and leaves of all the trees around me.

Cork, as I heard him called, began, "Bur oak twigs are stout, yellowish brown, and become *pubescent* after their second year." "UH, UH, UH," a small tree on the front row jumped up and down with excitement. "What's pub-scent?" Chuckles floated through the crowd like ripples on a pond.

"OK, who wants to explain to this curious youngster?" Cork bellowed!

One of the trees next to the questioner replied cautiously, "I think that's hairy,

isn't it? Or at least that's what my cousin tells me."

"Absolutely," said Cork, "so we know our twigs are big, yellow-brown, and pub-es-cent or hairy. Does everyone see that?" A rush of cool air wafted through the crowd as all the trees shook their tops while examining their twigs and their neighbors. I noticed Cork emphasized the correct pronunciation without making the young one feel bad about mispronouncing the word. Very kind, I thought. Pub-es-cent, wow, what a word. Glad I'm not in a spelling bee! Ahem!" Cork began, "Let's continue. We have much to learn and so little time. When the second year begins, our smooth twigs develop corky ridges." Cork pointed to the definitely corky ridges along its lower branches. OOOHs and AAAHs filled the air. The youngest saplings turned to inspect themselves and each other.

Cork continued, "Another detail to make note of is our buds. At the ends of our twigs, they are *clustered*. Who knows what that means?"

Up jumped a whip, anxious to share its

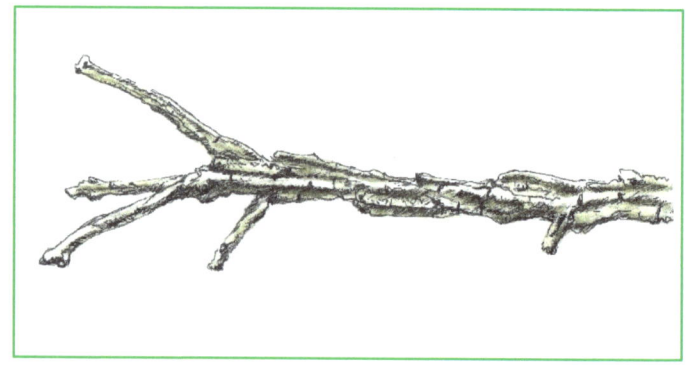

knowledge. "It means there's more than one bud at the tips of our branches." A larger bur next to the whip beamed so much I could hear the bark crack!

Cork was pleased as well. He patted the young whip on her leafy canopy. "Yes, said Cork, "and those buds are called "*terminal*" because they are at the end of the branch. Now, find those buds and tell me what you see around them?"

Examinations began in earnest. Saplings checked themselves and each other and shrugs of dismay came from every corner. I tried peering over limbs to get a look at the buds myself. I tapped on my neighbor's "shoulder", requesting a peek. As I scrutinized the buds sitting in a cluster at the end of the branch, "*terminal* buds", is that what Cork called them? I noticed little hairs sticking out from around the buds. I poked my neighbor and showed him what I found. Suddenly, I realized that they could not only see me, but they responded to me for the little sapling looked at the buds I pointed out, smiled at me, and wriggled his way to the front of the group.

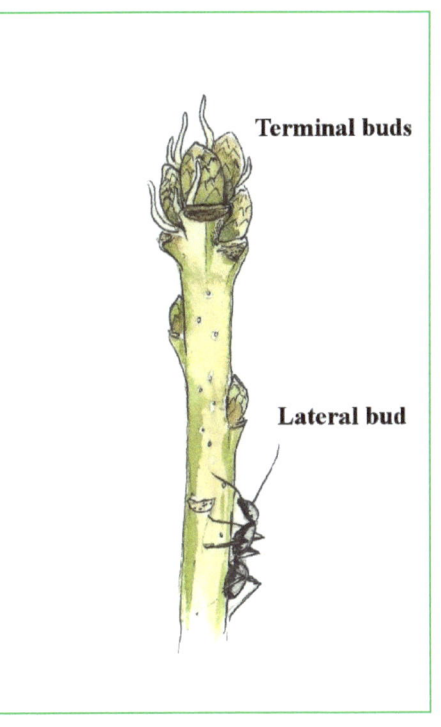

"I found them, I found them!!" he said with glee.

"Well, well, I believe we have a winner!" laughed Cork. "Tell everyone what you've discovered."

"Little hairs are all around my buds," was the proud statement.

"Great discovery, little one," said Cork with a wink in my direction. "Little hairs around our buds are a unique characteristic of us as bur oaks. Few trees have that trait. We should be proud!" Cork lifted his canopy and was filled with pride as were all those around me. My little neighbor danced with glee, giving high twigs to everyone as he strode back to stand next to me.

"I have another question for one of you in the front row," Cork beckoned to the spindly ones. "Now, that we know more about our *terminal* buds. What about the buds along the sides of our branches? What are they called?"

A quick twig was raised. "Momma and Poppa say they are *laterals*!" the sapling responded with much assurance.

"How correct you are, and brave to go out on a limb answering with such speed," chortled Cork. "These *lateral* buds along the sides of your branch are smaller than the *terminal* buds. But, wherever they're located, you can be very sure they're mostly *obtuse* and *tawny pubescent* like the *terminals*," Cork stated with a look of pride.

Behind me I heard a shrill, "What's *obtuse* and *tawny*?" Muffled chuckles filtered through the crowd. An older bur bent down and whispered to a tiny tree, "We'll look those words up when we get home."

"But, I want to know **NOW**!" pleaded the little one. "Etch your question onto this parchment and I'll explain as soon as Cork is finished." Furious scraping sounds along a small, thin piece of bark followed as the young sapling worked with the intensity of an ancient scribe to permanently display her question for later answers.

"Young whips are rightfully curious," I overheard an elder bur on my right whisper over my head to a tree on my left.

I turned to look at the "whip" they were speaking of and quickly made note that this tree was much smaller than the saplings in the front row, about an inch in diameter I guessed. So the smallest are whips and the next in size are saplings. Good information! I'm sure my editor will love this.

alternate branches

"Speaking of branching," Cork bellowed to focus their attention on the primary purpose of the gathering. "Let's compare ours to the human amongst us."

I whipped around to face the front. Cork was moving my way! When his roots were settled next to me, two of his massive branches lifted both my arms to shoulder height. "All of you burs lift your branches like the human has done," Cork instructed.

The sound of branches moving in unison was reminiscent of the night I watched the midnight train roll past the rural crossing near my parents' home in upstate New York. Calm, quiet and then a deafening roar!

"Aha!! Something's different. What is it?" questioned Cork.

Everyone looked at themselves, each other, and then at me. Aside from the fact that they were trees and I was a human, the differences escaped me.

Suddenly a young sapling blurted, "They're arranged differently!! The human's arms are straight across from each other and our branches aren't!"

A collective sing-songy OOOOH was heard throughout the gathering.

"How right you are! Our branches are *alternate*," Cork replied. "That means they are not on the same plane. The human has *opposite* arms. Most tree species have *alternate* branching, but some trees, such as our cousins, the maple and the ash, are like this human with *opposite* branching." I felt at once so very different from the burs, but at one with the *opposite*-branched trees. I resolved to find some when I got home. I scribbled more notes.

"Back to buds!!" Cork loudly proclaimed. "The branches stem from buds." Cork began to chuckle with delight at his own jokes. "Seriously," Cork tried again but the shaking of his leaves made it difficult to believe proceeding was on his mind. "There are other types of buds with different purposes," Cork began again. "*Flower* buds contain the beginnings of flowers. Then there are *mixed* buds comprising flowers and leaves."

"It must be very crowded in there," I overheard a young whip say to another while inspecting his branches. "No wonder they explode in spring."

"Boom!" said his neighbor while several young saplings chuckled nearby.

Cork's bark creaked with an obvious frown while he was peering in the direction of my neighbors. I guess only large oaks get to make jokes.

"BUDS and BRANCHES!" Cork shouted. "Branches that form from *terminal* and *lateral* buds are strongly attached to the tree for they start growing from the beginning of the development of the branch. They are connected to the larger branch or trunk deep into the heart of the wood. One of Cork's gnarly branches quickly reached out to a limb on a tree nearest him and gave a mighty tug! The surprised owner lurched forward! "STRONGLY attached!!" he said, repeatedly pulling on the

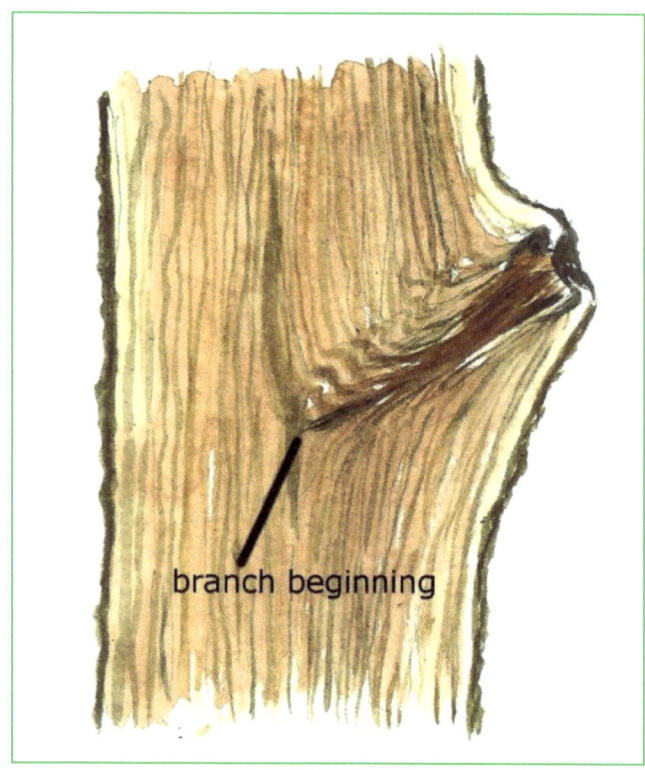

branch beginning

branch. "Because that's where our *terminal* and *lateral* branches start growing; deep inside, beginning when we are less than one year old."

"Yikes!!" squealed the bur whose branch was the object of our discussion. He slithered backwards, holding it close to his trunk, fearing Cork's reach and more pulling.

"Now," Cork continued, "there's still another type of bud called adventitious or dormant that forms just under the bark anywhere on the tree. If a branch forms from one of those buds and I pull on it, CRACK! It's easily pulled off because it is not strongly attached! It doesn't form deep inside. DEEP INSIDE!" He bellowed and pointed to his insides.

"Branches formed from these adventitious buds are accidental," continued Cork. "They form on our newest wood, the wood right under the bark which is usually due to wounding. After the wounding, the tree begins to make callus tissue to close over the wound and the dormant buds right under the bark take this as an opportunity to begin making branches. Since this attachment doesn't start deep inside, the branch is weakly attached."

"How does this wounding occur?" I whispered to my neighbor. Sound carries well, I discovered, or Cork had microphones planted in the group for Cork immediately responded, "Who asked that?" A flurry of branches pointed my way. "Thanks!" I muttered, eyeing all near me.

"Well, now those pointing at our human can provide some answers," said Cork.
I tried to conceal my gratification, but the smirk on my face was obvious.

"Storms?" The sapling next to me offered reluctantly. Cork's face cracked again, but this time with a wide grin. "How right you are! Storms cause branches to snap off and bark to be torn away. Then the tree begins to repair itself."

I believe the sapling's shoots grew a foot at that moment, with obvious pride in his answer. Older trees winked and branches nudged bark to bark as their pleasure showed in the young one's response.

"Are there other ways that wounding occurs?" Cork continued to query.

Several groups began to whisper amongst themselves. Some branches pointed my way. I was feeling a bit uneasy. I soon learned why.

"HUMANS!!" wailed an old bur in the background moving my way. "Humans!" he continued as his strides quickened.

I was looking around in search of an escape route, when two middle aged burs stepped between the charging bur and me. "Stormy", I now call the sapling at my side, joined them to protect me.

"It's not **this** human's fault." I heard one bur gently whisper to the older, enraged one. The old bur paused, looked at the others, straightened up, and strode away from me. One of the intervening burs placed a twig on my shoulder and nodded its canopy slightly. Stormy grew closer and wrapped a tiny twig around my leg. I looked down and mouthed, "Thank you."

Wounding? The enraged bur seemed to connect me to it. What did my protectors mean, "It's not THIS human's fault?" Quickly my mind ran back to last week when a group of kids skipped down my street stripping little branches from young trees. I never thought of this as a big issue. Perhaps, I have much to learn, as I brought out my paper and pencil to make notes of this increasingly complex system of trees.

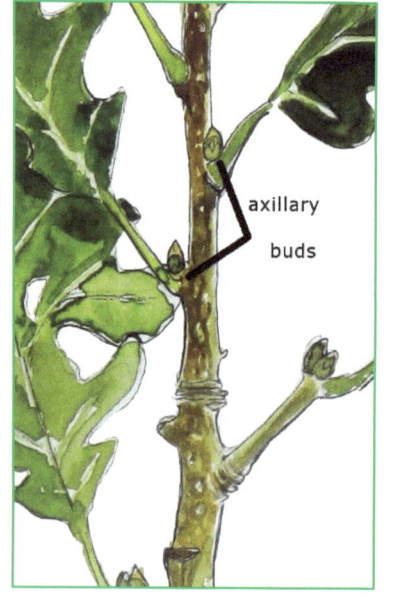

"LEAVES?" questioned Cork. "From where do they develop?"

I sensed Cork's desire to turn our attention away from the interruption, and I was brought back to the present, but I wanted to know more about what provoked that bur's response. Maybe later I would discover the answer, though I had some doubts that I wanted to hear the truth.

"Leaves!!" Cork stated again. "Where do they begin?"

Intense activity began. Heavily leaved branches were lifted and inspected. Sherlock Holmes himself couldn't have waged a better investigation. But, I heard no response. It seems no one knew the origin of their leaves.

Cork's crown shook from side to side. "I am amazed. You hold your lovely, leafy canopies so proudly, but don't know how they begin. Look closely at the base of a leaf. My dear friend, Lobelia, will dig deeper into your leaves, but for now we'll do a little examination. At the base of every leaf where it attaches to the stem is an *axillary bud*. Next year's twigs **and** leaves open from there."

Astounded OOOHs swirled through the air.

Cork's bark creaked and groaned. "All this *terminal, lateral, axillary, dormant,* and *adventitious* bud talk leaves me weary. That's a lot for an old bur. I need to rest now."

Burs continued to investigate themselves and their neighbors' leaves. I had to laugh, for their inspections reminded me of my cub reporter days at the Toronto Zoo watching baboons pick insects off each other. I chuckled with reminiscence as I worked my way to the rear of Cork's group and out into the grounds. While wandering, I frantically scrawled my thoughts of the morning's activities on my cellulose paper with a wooden pencil. Then, I became aware of an uneasiness with which some burs eyed me. The watchful glances and nods of a few apparently friendly patrons acquired at Cork's group seemed to dispel the crowd's fears. I decided, however, to switch to my fine-point Bic pen and write-in-the-rain paper, which consists of more cotton fiber than wood fibers. I hoped it would ease their fears and signal my desire to be accepted. It appeared to work, for many trees gently tapped my shoulders or tousled my hair as they passed me. I felt like a member of a football team who'd made a good catch.

As I watched them move away, I overheard the young whip in Cork's group who wanted to know about *pubescent, tawny and obtuse* say with impatience, "Now can you tell me!!" His father, patiently said, "Hold up your twig. Take a look at your buds.

Do you see those very tiny short hairs? Remember what Cork said. That's *pubescence*. Now, *obtuse* is a shape. It's rounded with no point." The young one nodded vigorously, beginning to see tree characteristics in a different way. "But what about *tawny*," he squealed?

"*Tawny*," pondered the elder tree, "is a golden yellowish-brown color, something like the hide of a deer. Beautiful isn't it?"

The little whip beamed while looking closely at his golden buds. "I am beautiful, aren't I?" "Yes, and that's why we're here. There are many reasons to feel proud of ourselves," beamed his father.

Chapter 3 - Ashley's Growing Pains

"I am older than you!!" "No, you're not!!" I spun around to hear a heated debate and scuffling between two young whips. Larger trees shuffled over to intervene.

"There's no reason to argue like this; it's easy to see who's the oldest," said an approaching bur.

Gasps could be heard from the by-standers. "She's going to cut them down and read their rings!" The crowd shuddered and yelled. "Ashley Oak, don't do it!" A huge guffaw bellowed from this moderately large bur. "That's not what I'm going to do." Ashley's large branch motioned for the two arguers to move closer. Gingerly they obeyed.

"Hold out your branches," instructed Ashley Oak. "Now look at your *bud scale scars*." They looked at their shaking branches with wide eyes and then at Ashley with considerable suspicion.

"What is the matter?" said Ashley grinning, "Can't you find them?"

"Find what?" replied the two young ones still shuddering with fear.

bud scale scars

Actually, I noticed they were not alone in wonderment. Many older trees were searching their branches for *bud scale scars*, too. I began to grin. Then a neighboring tree gave me a slight nudge with his branch and said, "What's so funny? Let's see your *bud scale scars*." I immediately cancelled my smirk.

Ashley overheard and let out a deafening laugh. "Humans don't have *bud scale scars*. They don't even have *terminal* buds." This little joke apparently touched everyone's funny twig, for waves of giggles infected the entire crowd. It was several minutes before calm returned to the group.

Finally Ashley continued, "Branch growth occurs yearly from *terminal* buds located at the ends of every branch. A covering of *bud scale*s protects the bud and in spring the bud opens, the scales fall off, and the branch grows. POOF! Like magic! It happens year after year. Everyone," Ashley **boomed**, "look at your neighbor's branches and share a branch with our visitor."

Suddenly, twigs appeared all around me. Many tiny peals of laughter could be heard as adjacent bur's twigs appeared under my arms, through my hair, and even in my ears.

"Attention, attention!!" Ashley grinned with delight.

"Find a bud, then notice a circle going around your stem.

That's the *bud scale scar*! You young ones can tell your age by how many times the *bud scale scars* appear on your twigs."

"How about counting them?" Ashley inquired, "Anyone?"

I could hear plenty of numbers adding up. "I'm four, I'm five, and I'm seven!! Wow, this is fun!! See, I am older than you!!!"

"What's all this space between *bud scale scars*?" questioned a medium sized bur in front of me. "Is there a name for everything?" I could see the region in question. It reminded me of the area between my elbow and wrist. I raised my arm for an inspection and a young sapling beside me placed a twig next to my arm. We looked down at our appendages. Then his bark creaked with a shy grin. The similarity was striking. I wiggled my fingers in response and my sapling friend wiggled a few leaves. I grinned and winked at another new found friend. "The spaces between buds are called *internodes*, and yes, there is a name for everything." Ashley stated with exactness.

"Do you have a "code" in your node?" laughed a jokester on the front row.

Ashley turned with mild displeasure, yet chuckling. "I believe that belongs to our human." I reached for my nose and bark splitting laughter began everywhere. It was so infectious I joined in.

"Remember, the place on your twig," Ashley continued, after regaining her composure, "where leaves are attached is called a *node*, and the area on the twig that's between the leaves or *nodes* is called the *internode*."

"AAAACCHOO! AAAAACCHOO! We all have colds in our nodes!!"

The young ones were at it again. If burs could roll on the ground from laughter, they would have looked like bowling pins shaking after a strike. I had to admit they were having fun learning.

"Young burs!" Ashley's booming voice straightened everyone up. "We have much to learn in our short time together. Remember, you carry the story of how you are made back to your neighbor burs back home."

I noticed one of the whips involved in the original "I'm Older than You" debate looking puzzled. Her bark scrunched together top to bottom and side to side. "But, Ashley wait," she said. "If big trees grow bigger around every year, what happens to the branch growth? How come the old ones can't tell how old they are from their branches?"

"Superb observation!" Ashley boomed with delight as branches waved madly. "What happens to your leaves every year?" Ashley inquired of the curious one.

internode

"They fall off!" the whip proclaimed proudly.

"Correct, and so do some branches." Ashley continued. "So counting *bud scale scars* in older burs might not be accurate!! It's the aged ones who can only tell their age from their rings." UUUUWWWs were heard from every corner of the group!!

I was puzzled by this response and looked at my neighbor who made the proverbial slash across the throat but at its middle. "EEEWWWWWWW!" I responded. I wondered what these rings were about. Maybe I'd learn more at a later stage.

"Back to branch drop, which occurs in most tree species, another way trees are the same and yet at the same time very different. A stunning mystery! Sorry, I have fallen from our original story. Where was I? Oh yes, my friend Lobelia will cover leaves in detail, but for now I'll just say that small branches drop from larger limbs in the same way leaves fall. The process is called *abscission*. You'll understand this perfect puzzle after hearing Lobelia." Ashley was silent as if the stories were complete.

Whispers and murmurs erupted in little pockets throughout the crowd. I looked at my new sapling friend, I'll call him Internode. "Are we through?" I questioned. Internode shrugged his branches, twisted his facial trunk, and rolled his eyes around with wonderment as well.

Finally, a mid-size bur spoke up. "Excuse me, Ashley, there seems to be something missing."

"Oh, is there?" Ashley pondered. "What could that be?"

"Twig growth makes us taller, but how do we grow in girth?" the bur questioned.

I chuckled to myself. My Uncle Jeff would have known the answer to that one. Let's see: pizza, ice cream, and cheese -- all the right stuff made HIM grow in girth!

"Rings!" Ashley blared while shaking a giant branch into the air with great drama. "Rings!" was repeated as she focused toward the sky. The entire crowd waited and looked skyward. The expectancy was as thrilling as waiting for Santa to descend the chimney. Any moment, I knew something would happen. Usually I munch a cookie at such a time, but nothing was left of my lunch.

So there's more about rings? My interest was piqued.

Earlywood and *latewood* – these ARE the answers!" Ashley stated with much

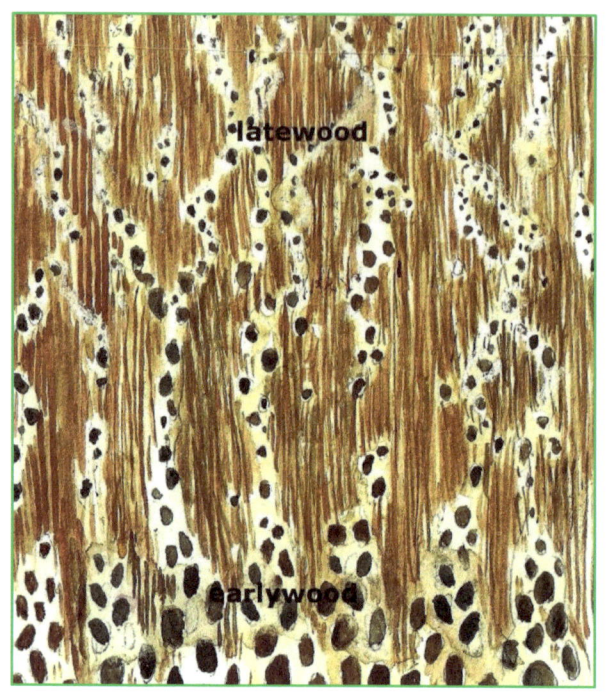

theater. I looked around for Sir Lawrence himself. Surely this was a Shakespearean audition. Ashley shuffled to the far end of the "stage" as I was now viewing events and turned slightly forward as if begging for a soliloquy. "Yearly growth occurs in two parts. Inside our trunk are two types of vessels like tubes moving water and nutrients from our roots to our leaves. Another vessel moves sugars from our leaves to our roots. Large vessels are produced early in the growing season, hence the name *earlywood*. Later in the season, *latewood* vessels are produced. These are considerably smaller." Spinning quickly around to face the front, Ashley blurted. "WHY do you think these large vessels occur in the *earlywood*? HMMMM??" The crowd was silent and everyone's eyes shifted from side to side, looking for an answer which reminded me of searching for my brother Craig while we were playing hide and seek.

Ashley straightened and propped her lowest branches on the middle of her trunk. "Think, think, think," she gently prodded. "What happens in the spring growing season?"

"OOH, OOH, OOH! I know!!" Internode was jumping with joy."Yes? Young one, what do you think?" asked Ashley.

"In the spring, I'm growing fast and I need to take up lots of water and nutrients from my roots. So I have large vessels to do that," the young one replied.

The applause was thunderous. My sapling friend turned as red as a sugar maple on a Connecticut hillside. Ashley beamed as well.

Internode paused and looked thoughtful. "What about the *latewood*, what is it for?" "My, my, I think you should be in my advanced class, such inquiring questions!

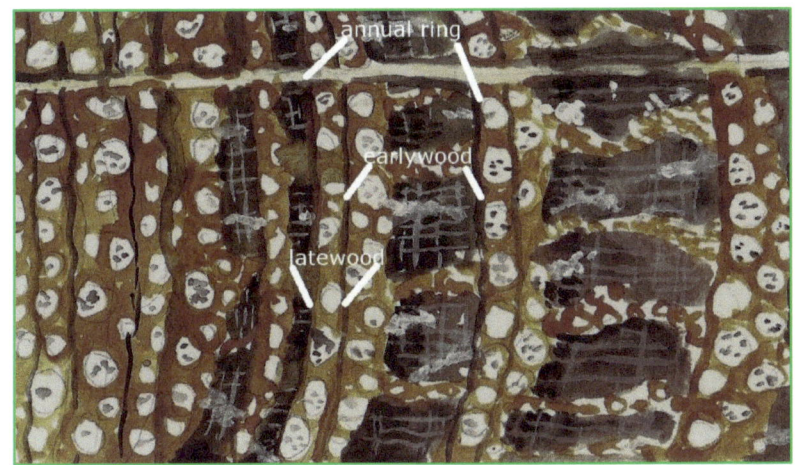

Does anyone have an answer?"

Without thinking I blurted out, "In the fall there's less moisture and growth so the vessels are smaller because they won't be sucking up much." "Incredible!" laughed Ashley. "My job is complete! Even the human is learning! Good Night, all!"

I said, "Wait, Ashley! What do the rings have to do with annual growth?"

Ashley turned to the group. "Can anyone answer the human's question?" "Do we add a ring of *earlywood* and *latewood* each year?" squeaked Internode with trepidation.

The crowd erupted with waving twigs, branches and cheers.

Ashley beamed and bowed in agreement. As she marched off with a great flourish and to tremendous applause. This time everyone was satisfied.

So that is the significance of the rings and annual growth. I was intrigued with everything, but the connection between leaf and branch *abscission* was a curious one. Is that the word -- *abscission*? I must have been muttering aloud, for Internode answered me.

"Yes, *abscission* is what happens to leaves. Are you going to hear Lobelia next?"

"Yes, I believe I will. There is so much to learn and so little time." Visions of the White Rabbit scurrying around Wonderland flashed through my head. Where is my watch?

Chapter 4 - Lobelia's Leaf Tales

After recovering from Ashley's twig tale, I spied a gathering of equally eager listeners under an ancient bur oak whose giant limbs spread 200 feet across the landscape. I was in awe of its size and grandeur. The sheer beauty and strength of the branches drew me below its crown. Many young burs had found their way to the front and as I forged ahead I heard one in the crowd asking questions of the giant tree.

"Lobelia, why do my leaves turn a golden yellow in the fall, but the leaves of other trees turn bright red?" a mid-sized bur standing proudly on the front row questioned.

An enormous grin cracked across Lobelia's bark. "Our leaves are very 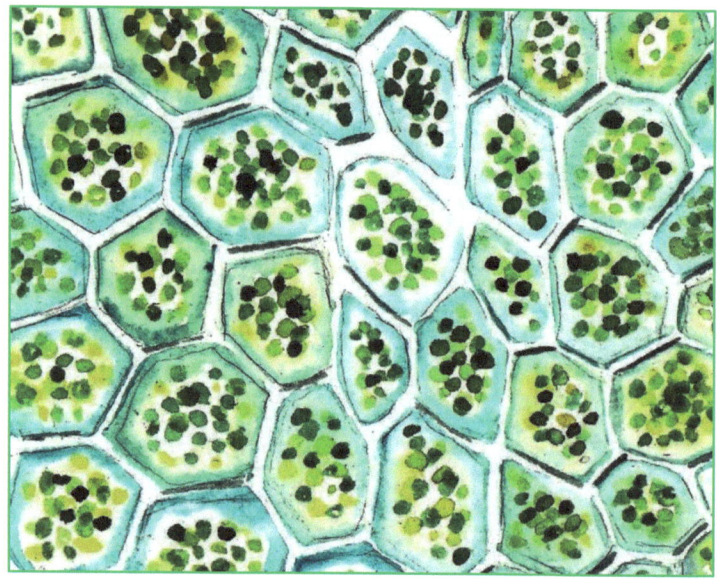 complex and composed of many cells. Inside each of the cells are hundreds of tiny *organelles* called *chloroplasts*, which contain *chlorophyll pigment*, she said with her lilting voice.

"*Organelles*, is that for playing marching music?" chuckled a marching sapling behind us. Lobelia didn't look very pleased with the interruption, but realized more explaining was necessary.

"Every living thing, even our human, has cells throughout our systems and inside these cells are pieces or *organelles* that when put together like a large puzzle keep us alive. One of the *organelles* in our cells is a *chloroplast*. Can everyone say that?"

"Chlor-o-plast", we all responded.

"Correct, and that *organelle* is green most of the time. During the summer, this green color or *pigment* is responsible for *photosynthesis*. Without this we could not remove carbon dioxide from the air, mix it with water from our roots and in sunlight, turn all that into *carbohydrates*." Ashley chimed in with a flourish. "Each of our leaves is a tiny factory pumping *carbohydrates* to every cell. Quite simply, if the factory quit working, we would die," she stated with a wavering voice.

Gasps of shock created a shudder that rolled through the crowd like the beginning of a gentle spring thunderstorm. A young one regained her composure and inquired, "But that still doesn't tell us how our leaves turn a beautiful, golden-yellow color in the fall."

With eyes gleaming in delightful mischief, Lobelia responded, "Ah, the yellow is always there."

"No, it's not," said an impish youngster.

Lobelia continued, undaunted, "Yes, it is, but it's masked or hidden by the green *chlorophyll*. During the summer our leaves are green, but when the short days and cool nights of autumn begin, the yellow or carotene *pigment* that's hiding in the *chloroplast*s begins to shine through. The green *chlorophyll* disappears and our golden yellow colors are displayed beautifully throughout the forest."

A couple of young saplings began swaggering around giving "high leaves" to each other. "Burs are cool! Burs are cool!" they chanted. Lobelia interrupted their gaiety, "Other tree species show beautiful, colorful pageantry in the fall, too. Behind the *chlorophyll* in other trees are *pigment*s of red, orange, and purple."

All around me, canopies shook in agreement that other trees also have beauty.

"What happens after our leaves change color?" shouted a bur.

"That is a spectacular mystery!" Lobelia mused with pleasure.

"Autumn brings days with less light and cooler temperatures and changes beyond color begin to occur within our leaves. Look at a leaf. Do you see where your leaf attaches to your branch?" A giant whooshing sound accompanied their positive response as canopies waved front to back.

Lobelia continued, "Another cell job begins. A layer of cells form at the base of the leaf where it attaches to the stem and it's called the *abcission layer*."

"Bless you!!" shouted a few burs. Then Lobelia gave a creaky grin, "I didn't sneeze; the cell layer is called *ab-ciss-ion*. These cells start cutting off water and nutrient flow to the leaf which causes it to wither, die and begin to make its way to the ground. This happens with some small branches, as well. I'm sure Ashley mentioned that process to you."

"It's been cut off!" a tiny whip yelled while clutching its bark in an imitation of strangling. Suddenly gasping, thrashing whips were flailing themselves across the forest floor.

Lobelia half-turned toward the self-amused display and squinted with mild displeasure and a half-grin. "Drama school is down the hill!"

We all chuckled.

A voice from the rear squealed, "Lobelia, a bur's yellow color makes our leaves special. Is there anything else about our leaves that make us unique?"

Lobelia exploded with delight, lumbered toward the tiny voice and picked her up with a light squeeze. "MY, MY YES!! I was hoping someone would be inquisitive enough to ask more questions. Come with me!" Lobelia carried the beaming, miniscule sapling to the front row, set her down, and sighed. "There's so much. Where shall I begin? AH, Yes! Everyone, pick up your branch and look at your leaves. What do you see? You in the back, tell me something about your leaf."

A tall, thin tree directly behind me shouted,
"My leaf, actually all of them, is attached to my twig by a smaller twig."

"That twig holding the leaf to the twig," remarked Lobelia," is called a ***petiole***. The *petiole* allows our leaves to move freely in the wind, creating cool winds below the canopy." "Cool!" snapped a whip to its neighbor. "Whoosh, whoosh through the air!" The two young ones wandered through the crowd imitating trees fluttering in a hefty wind - coincidentally pausing right over my head and fanning me to the amusement of everyone.

"AHEM, AHEM," Lobelia quietly nudged them and my neighbors back to reality.

"Returning to the question of what makes us different. Our leaf size, shape, margin, and *lobes* make us a truly unique species," continued Lobelia with obvious pride.

"I don't understand *margins* and *lobes*," whispered a sapling to the strong tall bur standing nearby who shook its canopy negatively. Frankly, I didn't either. I knew margins were at the edges of my paper, and my ears have lobes. But, I didn't think that was what Lobelia meant.

Lobelia overheard the question and continued the tale. "Margin is the edge of the leaf. It's like tracing a river's course. You follow along the waterway moving high into the mountains and then deep down into the valleys. Those are our lobes. Hold up a leaf and follow the edge. You'll see at least seven lobes and some of you have eleven. It's OK to be a little different. You're still a bur!"

Lobelia's voice chimed as the burs raised their leaves, inspecting each lobe. The variation in lobes was clear to me. Those with the most lobes proudly showed them to their neighbors. However, ones with fewer lobes focused on their glorious green colors. I mused at witnessing their competitive spirit, so like having the best car or house. Inside we are all quite similar.

The young "whisperer" near me gently raised a twig. "Lobelia, what else is special about our leaves?"

Lobelia looked skyward as if in great thought. "Why, they're **obovate** in shape and generally their size is six to twelve inches long and three to six inches wide."

Several in the crowd laughed and pranced around saying, "I'm *obovate*, I'm *obovate*."

What a story this is going to be! My editor is going to love this, I thought, as I furiously took notes.

Lobelia sauntered over to the joyous group and with a snicker stated, "Exxx-plain **obovate**!"

As quickly as the "prancers" started their dance, they halted and whispered with bowed canopies, "UHHH!! Not sure."

"Anyone else care to try?" Lobelia quizzed the crowd. Silence was as loud as the seventeen year locust. "You ARE here to learn, remember. How about a pear??"

"A pair of what?" quipped a youngster.

Lobelia laughed loudly, "I meant a pear that is eaten." "Lobelia, are you trying to feed the human?" wisecracked another youngster and snickers filled the air.

"How ABOUT a pear?" Lobelia repeated bringing the group back to the subject. "Have you seen its shape? Slim at the top and large at the bottom. If you turn a pear upside down, it's large at the top and small at the bottom.

Look at your leaves. What do you see?" I watched the sapling in front of me. Her leaves were being inspected and twisted up, down, all around. The young sapling paced and scratched furiously on her bark and canopy obviously deep in thought.

Detective at work, I thought, taking in clues and figuring it out.

A crescendo of awakened enlightenment coursed through the crowd.

"I see it!" many shouted as lights of knowledge flickered like lightning bugs on a warm, June night.

"What else do you see about your leaves?" queried Lobelia. "Look at my leaf! It's, it's dark green and shiny on top," came a voice from the young sapling to my right! "And pale and fuzzy underneath," shouted another! "Wow, and the base of my leaf is rounded on the sides and pointed at the bottom!"

"Technically that's called **cuneate**," said Lobelia, who was now sparkling at the

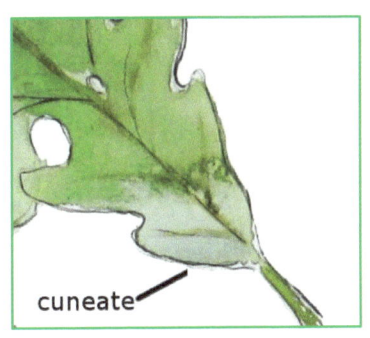

cuneate

new-found knowledge of the crowd. "THIS IS FABULOUS!!" Lobelia pealed with glee!! "Let's go back to *photosynthesis*. We've looked at our beautiful colors and shapes, but the glory of our leaves holds wonders beyond belief."

They were like putty in Lobelia's twigs, being molded and shaped with pride. The air was heavy with anxious anticipation.

"Remember, our leaves trap sunlight in the *chloroplast* and remove carbon dioxide from the air. A wondrous process occurs within our leaves to combine water and carbon dioxide and produce *carbohydrates* and oxygen. *Carbohydrates* are essential to our survival, and the oxygen produced is indispensable to humans." Lobelia stopped speaking and a calm quiet flooded the group. The mutual need between humans and trees was apparent. Respect for each other leapt upward like a spooked kangaroo. I looked around and inhaled deeply and exhaled as much as I could. It was a moment of pride for everyone.

"One other thing before we disperse:" Lobelia stated, "the importance of our leaves to the earth and soil around our roots. I'm sure you've heard about our vessels taking up nutrients from the soil, hmm?" Canopies shook in agreement.

"When I say our leaves fall to the ground and decompose after *abscission*, I mean that the leaves die, then fall apart or break down and the nutrients in the leaves are returned to the soil. At some point, these nutrients attach themselves to water and up they go again, flowing UP, UP, our **xylem** vessel to nourish us again."

"WOW! I didn't know that! Leaves are really important," I blurted out loudly. Lobelia gently nodded with pleasure. "Yes, it's like a puzzle. Even the smallest bits are an essential part of the

whole picture. With that I think I'll send you on to discover more of the puzzle." Thunderous cheers and hearty slaps on the nearest neighbors' trunks ended Lobelia's tale. I was tossed and twisted as my back and head became the target of many slaps.

The crowd moved in many directions and I overheard my two new sapling friends, Stormy and Internode, whispering, "Joseph is talking about how you can tell a juvenile tree from a mature one."

Internode replied, "Yea, I want to find out if I'm there yet. Ma keeps telling me I'm **not** sexually mature!"

I was equally mystified. "Trees sexually mature??" I said out loud. The two youngsters turned and waved for me to follow. How curious? I trailed quickly behind my new friends.

Chapter 5 - *Juvenility to Maturity or*
All You Ever Wanted to Know About Phase Change in Burs

It was easy to find Joseph, a tremendously old and big tree, surrounded by young saplings. If they were to root in place, not a ray of sun would hit the forest floor for the density of their crowns made light penetration impossible. I noted that interest in maturity is not strictly a human curiosity. It made me think of junior high study hall when one of my friends found a particularly interesting book in the library and we all gathered around to glean every morsel of information about becoming mature.

Peals of laughter and squeals broke my momentary reminiscence. The saplings were growing restless and louder in their anticipation. I grinned, noticing Internode and Stormy on the front row. "I can't wait to hear Joseph," he wiggled with delight. In the next instant, Joseph's voice boomed with such force that the leaves of the trees rustled and a hush fell upon the group. The silence was eerie. I had once reported from Charleston, South Carolina, when Hurricane Hugo hit, but this calm, quiet was unlike any other.

Joseph began, "Who knows what it means to be mature?"

Sapling stems waved in the air with frantic anticipation, but now their rush of leaves was akin to a gentle whisper. No words had yet been uttered, for Joseph commanded immense respect. Elders' eyes rolled as they peered around the area to see who had raised their branches.

Finally, Joseph eyed Internode and bade him to speak.

He began with a stammer, "I-I will be big and strong?"

Groans proceeded from the crowd. I cringed for the poor little guy.

"NO!" bellowed Joseph.

Now Stormy decided to attempt an answer, "My roots will be secure and I won't bend in the wind?"

Joseph frowned solemnly at this answer. Branches slowly bent toward the earth as the others suspected they didn't have the answers either.

"I think your parents have not informed you of the basics," growled Joseph. He scrutinized the older members of the species. Thick-leaved branches bent with shame. Muffled coughs were heard amongst the crowd.

"It has little to do with being big and strong, though that may happen when you are mature. But it is not a SIGN OF MATURITY," Joseph stated with intense deliberateness.

"Let me begin," Joseph stated with a calm, quiet demeanor. Tensions that had been slowly mounting were now released as a giant sigh engulfed our surroundings. But all were lulled into Joseph's mistaken calm.

For next came a boom, louder than the cannons in the 1812 overture. Surprise mixed with fear radiated from those closest to the front. I was glad I hadn't taken my place up there. I would have missed the looks on their bark. It was almost comical, since I knew my parents had never told me about maturity changes in humans either. I chuckled, thinking of my parents in a crowd of adults being chastised by Joseph. It was a funny thought.

I was again pulled back from my daydreams to hear Joseph's mesmerizing voice. "There are several external signs of maturity common to all tree species," he emphasized, "not just to bur oaks. One is so obvious and I suppose so commonplace that it is overlooked. A second sign is a trait used by humans in scientific research."

Gasps of terror were heard throughout the crowd. "Scientific research" whispered from one end of the group to the other. Joseph calmed their fears. "It does not involve the cutting of an entire tree, but using a portion of a young stem for rooting purposes." Relief was immediately noticeable throughout the older trees; however, the young saplings were not so assured. A few continued to tremble and grab their parents' trunks. Giggles began again, but were abruptly halted when Joseph leered in the direction of the offenders.

"The first sign has to do with spring. What occurs in the spring and is accompanied by a pleasant fragrance?" he queried the assemblage. One enterprising, but I fear cocky sapling replied, "Girls!!"

Snickers resounded throughout. Joseph looked slightly askance at the young one, but continued, "Not exactly! But you are on the right track." The sapling stiffened with surprise and pleasure.

"It does have to do with male and female parts of the tree."

"Oh boy! This is what I have been waiting to hear!" replied the sapling next to me, excitedly grabbing me around the neck. Thankfully he wasn't very strong and he quickly returned to his position of silent anticipation as Joseph continued.

"Male flowers appear as *catkins* and female flowers sit all alone or in groups of two or three on the current year's small branches or branchlets.

"Hold it, hold it," said the cocky, young bur. Did you say that the male and female flowers are on each tree? So I've got girl cooties on me? "

"I'm afraid so! But think of it this way: you don't need to travel far to find a date!!" Joseph laughed with delight. "Seriously," began Joseph, this is called '**mon-ecious**' or one–house, meaning that our male and female parts are located on one tree. Other trees are called '**di-ecious**' or two houses. That means it is either a male or female tree. Isn't that amazing!! "

I was lost in this new world and blurted out, "How do the male and female seeds get from one part to another?" Joseph was obviously proud of my involvement and stated, "Blowing wind and bouncing squirrels spread the pollen throughout our canopy AND the bees and butterflies flitting from flower to flower scattering our pollen from tree to tree. Without this process, seed formation would not occur."

"Wow!" I said and all laughed, even Joseph.

"Good to see you're in the spirit of the day," chuckled Joseph. "Now on with our seeds which are…," paused Joseph. Enthusiastic branches shook the air.

"Everyone in unison…" Joseph began, "Seeds are known as "ACORNS!" the crowd enthusiastically replied. Leaves and stems shook as many acknowledged they indeed knew THAT bit of information. Several OOOHs and rustling leaves could be heard from the younger set. There was almost a sign of relief among the oldsters, that finally Joseph had mentioned something familiar to their offspring.

The cocky youngster was not finished questioning. "How old will I be when I can make acorns?"

"Brilliant, Brilliant! I can tell you'll take my place when I move on to Bur in the Ground. Look around, does anyone have acorns forming?" Joseph replied with glee. "Well, who has an acorn?" he queried. A few of the whips and saplings checked themselves out with disappointment on their faces. Some of the medium-sized burs picked up their branches and shook them in front of the young ones with delight. They had acorns and wanted to show off.

"AHEM!" Joseph stated with a displeasing frown on his bark. "It wasn't that many years ago that you sat where the young ones are now."

The mid-size burs bowed their canopies low. "We were just showing them our acorns." One said trying to squeeze his way out of trouble.

"OK, nice try! " said Joseph, How old are you three?"

"Thirty-five, forty-two, thirty-seven!" shouted the mid-size burs.

"That's right," Joseph retorted, "burs must be at least thirty to thirty-five years old before they produce acorns. It's just a fact of bur life. There's a time for everything and age is one of the marks of maturity."

Groans could be heard from the little ones. "I don't want to wait. I want to be mature now."

Joseph laughed, "Everyone wants to grow up fast."

I had to chuckle, too. Boy, sounded just like me! I wanted to drive a car so bad when I was twelve. I hated waiting for someone to take me places. I was in such a hurry to grow up!! And then I got there and other things happened as well. Bills, bills, bills! I must have been muttering out loud for Joseph questioned, "Excuse me? What about bills?"

I shook my head and came back to the present. "Sorry, just day dreaming."

"Well, we will move on now to the second sign of maturity as I mentioned earlier," whispered Joseph, as the entire group bent forward straining to hear its every word, "but it is - not - as - in-ter-est-ing." The last few words proceeded with such slowness that I nearly fell on my face with the rest of the listeners as we leaned forward eager for every syllable.

"UH!!" came the surprised voices from the saplings.

"It is terribly important to the continuation of our species, however." he nearly growled in retort to the disappointed looks he received.

"Easy rooting," he quipped majestically.

I admit I was as puzzled as the rest. Shrugging of branches and shaking of leaves, stirred up clay particles on the forest floor. Several took to coughing and sputtering as Joseph calmly explained.

"Though this is rare, when wood is in the juvenile or immature stage, a broken branch can be placed in the ground and roots will form." Groans of pain went up as young and old grabbed their branches while visualizing Joseph's explanation.

"You know how rough the saplings and seedlings are to each other; loss of branches is inevitable. So while they are young, new trees could sprout from these losses. As we reach maturity, the ability of these branches to easily root is lost. That's why we must be careful as we age." Joseph spied a few elders that he had seen playing rough with the squirrels. They peered off into the sky, pointing at soaring vultures, pretending to have heard nothing.

"You really have nothing to fear," laughed Joseph, "for it is humans who've taken this juvenile quality and used it to develop new burs or other tree hybrids. I expect there are many other uses for this trait. It will take some in-depth explanations that I fear must wait for another time." Joseph began to yawn and stretch his enormous branches.

Several saplings grew uneasy fearing that Joseph was finished. They looked wide-eyed at each other. "Are there any other signs of maturity?" one sapling asked another.

An eager sapling raised his wispy branch.

"Yes?" inquired Joseph.

"What is the third sign, and is that all?" said the sapling with trepidation.

"Oh, yes, the third sign," Joseph pondered. "Withering!" he said with deliberateness.

"Huh?" was said in comical unison. It was like they were going to begin a song and someone had hummed the key of C. In fact, I chuckled a little too loudly and all eyes, including Joseph's turned my way. I coughed with embarrassment, as I murmured "I'm sorry" several times. I was really interested in this trait, and I surely didn't want to lose their confidence in me at this point. "Withered or dried leaves that remain through the winter. Have you noticed that?" queried Joseph.

Trees on both sides of me shook in unison. "Yes, but why?"

"It's a mystery of our species," stated Joseph. "But other trees, white oak and beech, for instance, also exhibit this juvenile characteristic. As the whole tree matures, the lower immature branches hold onto their brown withered leaves all winter.

Remember, I said these three traits are common to our species, but there are other signs of maturity unique to other tree species." "Like what," squeaked a seedling behind me? "Oh, thorns, for one," Joseph stated calmly. "OOH! Like who?" asked one standing near Joseph.

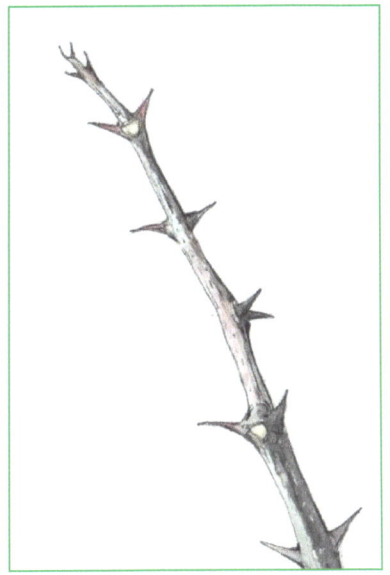

"Well, not an owl. That's for sure," Joseph chuckled, peering in the direction of the questioner. Laughter filled the arena.

"Black locusts," Joseph stated, "have thorns as a juvenile characteristic. In fact the black locust has both juvenile and mature phases on the same tree. The lower part of the tree may remain juvenile, bearing thorns and lacking the capacity to flower, after the upper part has attained maturity."

Joseph began to tick off other signs of phase change in rapid succession while I frantically wrote. I didn't want to miss a morsel of information.

"Leaves of sassafras are different shapes. Immature leaves are lobed and look like mittens with only a thumb, while others may have a thumb and one finger," Joseph continued.

One enterprising and inquisitive youngster queried quickly, "What's a thumb?"

Joseph laughed with glee. "That is a human feature. Next time you see one, inspect it." All eyes suddenly turned my way. I could see Joseph chuckling with delight. In fact his huge, thick branches moved up and down in a wavy motion as laughter continued in enjoyment of my predicament.

So, I politely held up my hands, not quite knowing what else to do. Threads of "OOOH!" worked their way through the throng as I wiggled my thumbs.

Joseph composed himself but worked to hold back his laughter and delight at seeing the look on my face. In the midst of the laughter, a yawn spread across his thick bark. "Enough for now," he said. His giant branches raised skyward stretching and yawning. "More stories tomorrow."

As the group dispersed, I overheard one elder say to her offspring, "We can find out more about rooting traits from Rooty. Tomorrow! Now to bed. Dream about birds, bees, and flowers tonight."

I, too, needed rest. The inquisitive little sapling who asked about thorns shuffled in our direction. Stormy and Internode motioned for "Thorny" to follow along. They took my hands and pulled me with them.

Stormy invited me to sleep at his camp. Upon arriving, various ages and sizes of burs gathered around, recounting their day's events. The name "Rooty" was repeated often. I anticipated hearing more intriguing tales tomorrow.

I leaned against a bur to continue listening to their stories with Stormy, Internode and Thorny curled up beside me and must have been very tired, for the next thing I knew, my nose was tickling. "Just a few more minutes' sleep, Maxx," I begged.

I flicked what I thought was the whisking of my golden retriever's tail across my face and opened one eye slightly to see three tiny trees smiling at me!

I rose up with a jolt having forgotten where I fell asleep. Internode, Stormy and Thorny were waving their leaves across my face and chuckling.

"Come on!!" chimed the three. "It's time. Tales are beginning."

They ran off to my left, waving for me to follow, but I spied something in another direction, and motioned for them to go on without me. Rooty beckoned.

Chapter 6 - Getting to the Root of the Matter

Running across the green, I discovered why this gathering of burs caught my eye. Their size drew me in. While the other groups consisted of seedlings, saplings and older trees, these were different, and my reporter's mind wondered why. As I made my way toward the crowd, I felt uneasy. I was sure I was being watched. I searched in several directions, but saw no one eyeing me like when I first arrived. For the most part, the bur clan had accepted my presence. I think replacing my wooden pencil with a ballpoint pen put them at ease. So, I couldn't understand my present wariness.

I shrugged it off as my eyes were drawn to the assembly surrounding an immense bur. The size of the tree was remarkable. I had been told that as burs age, the corky wings upon their branches increase in size and number. By the look of those branches, I would speculate this one was among the most aged.

The entire group, as I surmised from afar, consisted of larger and older trees. I approached with respect for I realized I was in the presence of the learned. In many human cultures, age and wisdom walk together and this appeared true here as well. This truth transcended the obvious physical differences between the burs and humans.

I found a spot near the rear of the assemblage, and prepared to be fed much wisdom. Again, that feeling crawled up the back of my neck. Who was watching me? And why? I looked around. Everyone's eyes were forward with intense anticipation of the stories to follow. I ignored my paranoia and hastened to listen. Cheers and applause were rising. "Rooty! Rooty!"

The voice from within the tree was deeply resonant. "Fellow burs, it is with sadness that we gather to discuss our roots," he began. "I look around and see the faces of my dear, old friends. I have known many of you from the time we were barely out of the acorn. Tell me, where are the little ones? Do they not have need to hear this message?"

One large tree from the back boomed, "It is not a flashy subject, like our shapely leaves, their golden fall color, or our deeply furrowed bark."

"Here, here!!" came echoes from across the crowd. An evangelistic surge was beginning.

"They don't understand the significance of our roots," another barked.

I had to admit I was mystified myself. What **was** so important about the roots? The age and fervor of the group led me to believe I had much to discover.

Murmuring began in small groups and soon the din was deafening. However, quiet overcame the crowd as the speaker's branches shook. It appeared to be a signal I would have missed had it not been for the response of the group. "We must persevere," the old one quietly began. "We are gathered in this place to remind ourselves of our common roots, but we must not forget to tell the story of our underground roots. Unseen is sadly forgotten."

There it was again, that feeling at the nape of my neck. I knew I was being watched, but from where? Everyone's eyes were riveted on Rooty. Who could it be? My thoughts wandered back to the growing enthusiasm of those around me, when I felt a tug at my pants leg. I looked down with surprise to see a very tiny sapling holding on to me. I could see a speck of brown out of the corner of my left eye. I **was** being watched. I reached down with my hand to touch the tiny, spindly appendage wound around my pants leg. It was Stormy!

Ever sat on your dad's foot, twisted your arms and legs around his calf, and held on for a ride around the living room? Picture a small tree entwined in the same manner around my leg. I gingerly lifted my left leg and the tiny tree lifted with me. I raised my foot a little higher and faster and giggling began. Just for fun I decided to run in circles. I wasn't sure who would give first. Motion sickness is my nemesis. To my surprise, the tiny tree tumbled off my foot and rolled to the edge of a small group of variously sized trees trudging past us. I laughed as my new friend rolled around at the base of those trees, flinging and bouncing as if this were a giant, outdoor pin-ball game. Those gathered around were laughing, too. It took me a moment to realize the laughter was directed at something else entirely.

My little friend was bound tightly by, appropriately enough, his roots. My stomach began to ache from laughter as I watched him twist and turn, trying to discriminate branches from roots. I became uncomfortably aware that the laughter was mine alone as a huge shadow stole my sunlight. **It was Rooty**, growing weary of our untimely display.

"HMMMPH!! Excuse me!!" he boomed. "May I be of assistance so I CAN CONTINUE WITH MY DISCUSSION OF OUR ROOTS!!"

I was terrified. In my fear, I tried to hide behind my little friend. Again we made quite a comical sight and twitters of laughter began anew. Papa Root spun so quickly in the direction of the new offending laughter, the trees standing near me fell

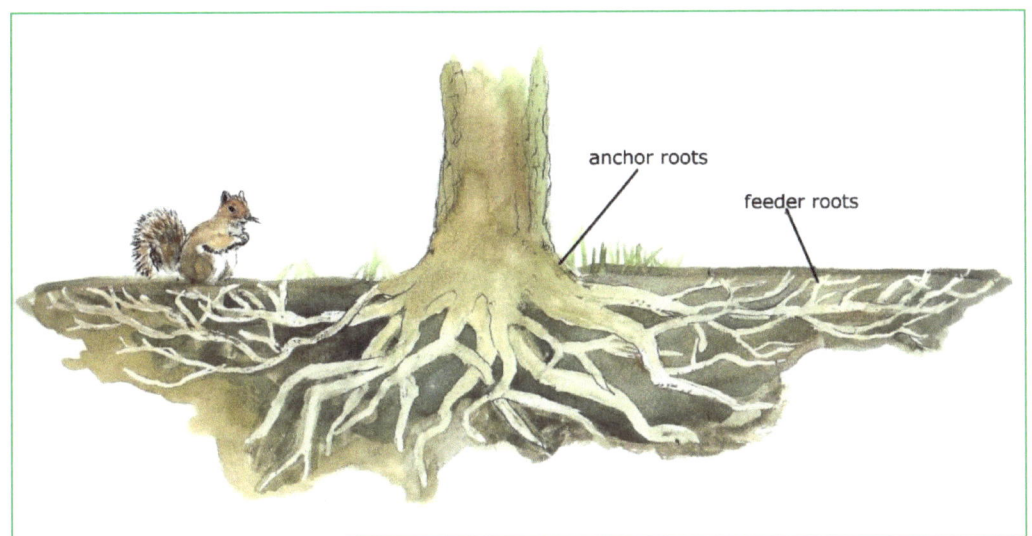

over like bowling pins. With this newest interruption, Rooty stormed to the front of the crowd and with serene whispers stated, "The matter of our underground roots is so fundamental to who we are, I can only suggest that those not interested -- **LEAVE**! Those remaining will be mystified!" With that comment, all in attendance came to attention. No one departed. Stormy and I decided it was time to pay attention. Rooty didn't say a word. We waited. We twisted. We wiggled.

"Please, tell us about our roots," a few voices began. "We want to know."

Now, spurred on by the imploring crowd, Rooty drew up proudly and proceeded as if nothing had happened to delay his discourse.

"Roots have specialized functions," he stated with a pause. Then motioning, he said. "Look at yourselves. Those heavy exposed roots extending from the trunk," he pointed down, "have a very special purpose. They keep us standing upright and balanced. As we grow taller, they grow broader and stronger. If it weren't for them, we'd topple."

I suddenly felt my arm thrust into the air. Rooty spied my odd arm waving madly. With scrunching brow I swear I could hear the bark crack around its large dark eyes.

"Yes? Is there something I can help you with, Thin Arm?" Everyone snickered at the apt description of my upheld appendage. I gulped, realizing my impertinence. I was silent. "Go on," he said with encouragement. Others nearby nudged me as if to push words from my mouth.

"I've seen trees in my neighborhood staked with wires to hold them up. Doesn't that work?" I asked. Gasps were followed by guffaws from all corners of the crowd. Rooty held up his branches to quiet the crowd. "Now, now, let's not discourage questions from the thin arm."

"I can see why from your experience as a human you would wonder about this common practice. Staking and guying a tree, however, prevents the natural process of strengthening our wood and growing our roots."

"Let me think, think, think. How to explain this? Hmmm! It's just like your form of exercise. Our roots' job is to anchor us to the ground. As the wind blows, the movement causes the wood in our trunks to strengthen. This in turn helps to make the roots stronger and longer. Movement sends a message to our roots so if our trunks don't move because it is prevented by staking and guying, our roots don't grow and they become weaker and weaker." I must have looked strange for Papa Root asked if I understood.

"I'm not sure I really understand." I admitted.

"Well, let me see." thought Rooty. "If you never moved your muscles or added extra weight to make your muscles work harder, you'd become weaker, right. So, moving in the wind doesn't hurt us anymore than exercise hurts you. Our roots work with our trunk to grow stronger and to anchor us more firmly in the soil."

With each word, Rooty inched in my direction, towering and bending over me. We were now squarely face to face. "Is it clear?" I shook my head up and down vigorously and glanced around sheepishly. I could see many middle-aged tree branches folded across their trunks and looking at me rather smugly, as if I should have known.

Rooty ambled toward the front and cleared his throat to call attention to the topic at hand and thankfully no longer on me. "Ahem," he coughed, "we shall continue. Roots have many functions. Our surface roots anchor us as I mentioned previously," he said with a sideward glance in my direction. "Then there are our feeder roots, whose importance cannot be overlooked."

A few younger saplings were beginning to filter into the crowd. One scooted in laughing and giving a "branch-bow" to its neighbor asking, "Is it feeding time?" Rooty overheard the chuckles. And turned ever so slowly toward the young ones and merely said, "Yes, it is, but do you know where and what these roots feed upon?" Several "Uhs" and "Wells" came from the young ones who just entered, but said nothing else. Rooty turned to the entire assembly that was enjoying the discomfort of the youngsters. "What about the rest of you? Can someone tell me about the feeder roots?"

Quizzically, confused faces turned toward each other. One brave branch fanned the air in response.

"W-water and nutrients," she responded nervously.

"CORRECT!!" boomed Rooty. "But there is one problem here. We don't actually feed. That's what humans do. We **soak** up what we need from the soil. Feeder or soaker roots are tiny and numerous. Here's another question," Rooty said with great delight. "Why is that important?"

I thought and thought. Rooty's question reminded me of my dog, Maxx, at bath time. Especially when he's finished bathing and I reap the rewards of his numerous hairs shaking water everywhere. "More roots, more water," I said out loud.

Even Rooty laughed at that one. "More water is absolutely right," he continued to chuckle. "The fine roots work their way through tiny cracks in the soil to search for more water and nutrients. It's an important role for these roots." "Is that all there is to our roots? " Stormy squeaked in my direction.

Rooty began to laugh and throw his branches up in the air, upon hearing the question. His laughter turned to tears streaming down his bark. "I never thought I'd hear a young one ask such an important question. Rooty began a chimed response, "*Root hairs! Mycorrhizae! ROOT HAIRS! MYCORRHIZAE!! ROOT HAIRS!*

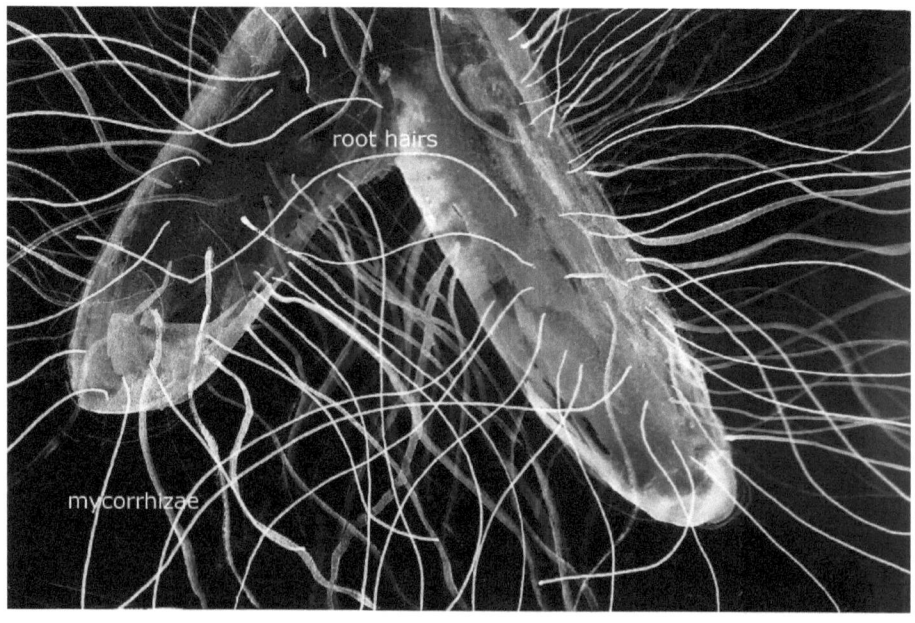

MYCORRHIZAE!" I thought it was a commercial for Root Grow! His evangelistic spirit grew with each phrase.

"Listen!! What you can't see is vital! Do you believe?"

The crowd was beginning to feel its fervor!

"Yes, yes!! We believe."

"Root hairs," he said, swaying and talking, "live such a short time."

Rooty seized on their attention. "Water, nutrients - the stuff of life. We couldn't live without them. Do you understand their importance? Thousands of miniscule root hairs attached to our tiny feeder roots absorb our life blood and then DIE." Rooty said with considerable emphasis. "Some live only a few hours. They perform their vital function and then become part of the soil. It's a hero's end." Rooty bowed and the entire crowd fell silent.

A quiet question rose from the crowd, "How many of them are there?"

"There could be thousands, even millions throughout our root system," Rooty expounded with passion.

"EEEEEEK!!"

A couple of young whips rushed toward the sudden shrill sounds of their neighbor.

I froze in fear at the horrifying sound, and then leapt forward as my reporter's heart took over. A story! Shrieks and gasps flew through the group and I saw young whips flying through the air. Then I heard barking! Barking, I couldn't believe my ears. "EEEEK!! WHAT is it??" shrieked the young bur looking at the ground.

A little brown and white beagle with its nose close to the ground stopped near a large, aged bur and began to furiously dig. I arrived on the scene to discover a black, globular shaped mass in the paws of the beagle. "What is it?" I questioned as the young ones scattered and hid behind larger burs.

"AHHH, *mycorrhizae*!" confirmed Rooty emphatically, "and a truffle."

"Mi - core?" I inquired. My pen was scribbling madly. "Could you please spell that? Is it dangerous? Should we evacuate? Do you have a plan?"

Rooty roared with laughter.

I paused to gain my composure. "OK, what is Mi-core-rrz?" I shrugged with perplexity showing all over me. "And that black glob in the ground, a truffle you say, what does it have to do with anything?"

"It's perfectly normal," Rooty declared with certainty. "Remember, I said there are two items important to our root system, root hairs and this, *fungi* and *mycorrhizae*." He pronounced it as if it was a dignitary entering the Oval Office.

"So?" I questioned with bewilderment."

"SO!!" Rooty proclaims with an astonishing pause. "What we have here is a failure to understand! My dear friend these globs, as you call them, are *truffles*, the fruiting bodies of our special partner, *mycorrhizae*. These *fungi*, as they are also called, are evidence of a great work occurring below the ground. The *fungi* produce a fine mat of *hyphae* or tissue that covers the surface of our roots and *mycorrhizae* are entwined with all of it.

"Hold it, hold it!!" I interrupted. "I thought *fungus* or mushrooms, as I knew them, were on top of the ground." Rooty explained, "The truffle is also a fungus, the special fruiting body for oak mycorrhizae, but it doesn't appear above ground, it's an *endomycorrhizae*, which means it is on the outside of the mycorrhizae but still underground. And would you believe it. People hunt truffles and eat them. That's why the beagle is here. He's looking for fungus gold!"

A few burs shouted about then, "I wish this truffle hunter would go away. He's not digging anymore, but looking at our bark funny and lifting his leg." I chuckled, thinking of Maxx!

Then I heard a few squirrels chattering and running through the canopies with the beagle close behind barking, chasing and being lead out of the forest.

Canopies fluttered in oak applause!

"Thank goodness it's gone, I have questions," squealed Stormy. "Why are these mycorr –i-zee important?" Rooty beamed proudly at the little one. "You are becoming very inquisitive. I like that. Think about it, young one! What do the *hyphae* of the mycorrhizae look like?" Rooty probed.

Stormy's canopy bent forward like Rodin's "The Thinker"; some serious pondering was occurring. Suddenly he bounded upward!

"They're like tiny roots. Lots and lots of them!! More roots mean more soaking ability. Our root system has increased."

"Superb!!" Rooty proudly rose up to his full height and beamed at Stormy. In fact, that reminds me -- our root system! How big do you think it is?" he asked quizzing the crowd now.

Stormy let out a deep sigh, relieved to be off the hot seat.

By now, Rooty had piqued the interest of the entire assembly. Without waiting for a response from the group, Rooty marched forward.

"Depending, and I mean depending on the soil conditions, whether it is dry, wet or in between, our roots spread horizontally two-three times our height." Rooty straightened up proudly.

"Wow!!" exclaimed the audience, including myself. I was impressed. I thought, however, about trees in the city with all the digging for houses, roads, and sidewalks. I shuddered, picturing what was happening to their roots. Oh, and I remembered the day I planted hostas at the base of my front yard tree. I hacked away at the roots, making way for plantings. I hope they can't read my mind. I cringed at the memory. I was brought back to the present by a quizzical youngster.

"Are we fast?" my little friend bravely asked Rooty. Older trees nearby grinned and tousled his tiny little leaf canopy.

"Juvenile roots are fast! Like everything else, young ones can't wait," Rooty chuckled. "Actually it's an important strategy. The seedling pops to the surface and the roots take off like rabbits running from the fox. The seedlings have a head start. In fact, a taproot forms before the first leaves unfold."

About that time a cloud of dust flew into our midst. "Did I hear someone say juveniles are fast?" exclaimed Internode as we coughed and laughed at his entrance.

Behind me came little tapping and giggling sounds on the bark of a tiny bur.

"What is going on?" Rooty bellowed to the astonished Stormy.

"Uh, helping our friends with their roots. You know, tap, tap, tap…..to help them grow." His answer was slowly becoming a whisper.

A few smirks were heard from the aged burs.

"That's not the *'taproot'* I meant." Rooty hid a slight chuckle himself. "A taproot is a single root that grows straight into the ground when the seedling starts to grow. It helps it stand straight while all the smaller roots begin to inch out into the soil." I swear the bark of the saplings changed color as they stopped their tapping. Rooty continued, "After one growing season, a seedling may have a taproot of over four feet and a mass of fine *lateral* or horizontal roots spread out over thirty inches.

"WHEW!!" whistled the large oak near me. "I hardly remember those days."

I looked down to find my sapling friends bursting with pride. They were willing themselves to grow through stretching and parading, something akin to novice body-builders.

"This ability is useful to us burs, because of where we live," Rooty continued. "Finding and absorbing water in prairies and other dry habitat is tough. We need ample roots, root growth, and root hairs, otherwise it will be difficult for us to compete with other species." At that moment Stormy and Internode punched at each other and the air, like mock prize fighters, but all they did was stir up more dust particles.

"So the deep-root myth is true?" I questioned through my coughing.

Rooty turned, strode my way and, placing one branch gently on my shoulder, stated firmly, "No, it's not universally true. It is, as you say, a myth. Our taproot disappears after a few seasons because it was there to help us in our early years. For most mature forest trees of a variety of species, the feeder roots are in the top eighteen inches of the soil and spread out way beyond the shadow under our canopy. This deep-root myth leads to serious problems, especially for trees living in cities. It is very sad. You may have an opportunity to witness the results first-hand while you are here."

I sensed my question fell on a heavy heart and I was sorry I mentioned it. Then I wondered what was meant by "first-hand"?

Rooty returned to the front and addressed the waiting audience. "Our roots are vital to our existence! We must spread the message! Radiate from here! Broadcast what you have learned! We must not give up!"

Rooty ended amidst a thunderous applause of waving branches and leaves, mounting cheers, and a standing ovation. However, I'm not quite sure how one could tell; I thought they were already standing. I stood and loudly applauded, feeling a bit inferior with only two appendages to wave and clap while showing my deep appreciation for Rooty's wonderful saga.

The crowd enthusiastically dispersed in all directions, searching for more stories. Internode ran off in one direction and Stormy was off in another. The older burs tapped their bark, showing approval of participating with Rooty. I held back a bit, surveying the possibilities. I, too, wanted more. A small red bird twittered melodically as it flew effortlessly above my head. Glancing in its direction, I noticed the beauty of the azure blue sky. There was music in the air. Literally, there was music in the air and I followed it.

Hmmmm!!!   HMMMMMMMM!

Hmmmm!!!   HMMMMMMMM!

Hmmmm!!!   HMMMMMMMM!

Harmony! Musical harmony! Like a barbershop quartet! I skipped toward the sounds. Several burs were holding court with many more gathering around. It was delightful to see and feel the harmony expressing itself in the responses of those around me. We all swayed to the pleasing sounds. *"Xy-y-lem, phlo-o-em,"* the chorus ebbed and flowed. Trees bent and moved to the music. I shifted back and forth to the sounds as if intoning a mantra. It was infectious, but I had NO idea what they were singing about.

The humming and swaying slowed. I spotted that same red bird flitting from tree to tree, twittering and alighting momentarily with the gentle shaking of a branch. I felt so peaceful; I sat on the ground at the base of my neighbor tree and wondered with pleasure what I was going to learn. A graceful, mid-aged bur separated from the harmonious group at the front. I whispered to the bur next to me, "Who is this?"

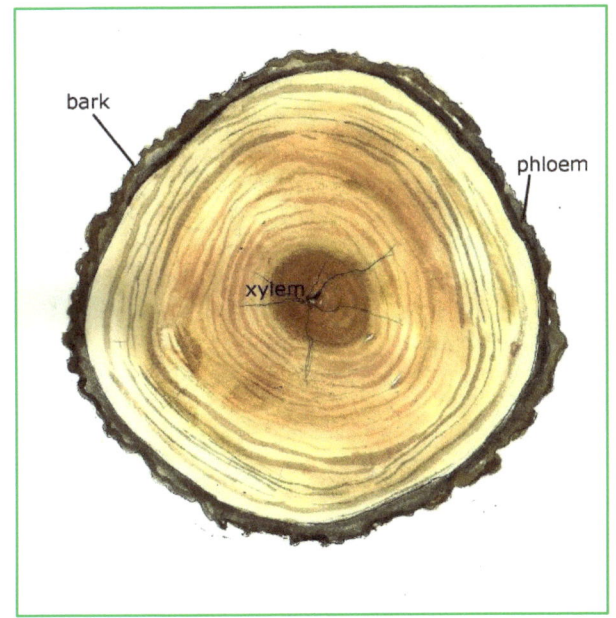

"Chloe!" was the quiet reply, "of the Inner Parts!"

OOH! And Wow! I thought.

"Xylem and phloem!" Chloe began gracefully. "A most harmonious system flows through each and every one of you! You can't have one without the other."

Can't have one without the other! I pondered that thought. Sort of a catchy phrase. I wonder if it could be from a song my parents sang. I was brought back to the present as Chloe continued singing and my neighbor tree moved to the side. I dropped onto my back and saw a friendly face grinning at me from above.

"I'm sorry for moving. I wanted to get closer," said my leaning tree. I grinned back and hurried to my feet to move forward with the group.

"As I was saying, the *xylem* and *phloem* are so important, that if either quits functioning or is damaged, **we are in jeopardy of dying**," Chloe stated with such intensity that everyone gasped in horror.

"How is that possible?" questioned my leaning tree.

Glancing around the assemblage, I saw a few brush tears away from their furrowed bark with their smallest leaves.

"*Xylem* and *phloem*", Chloe explained, "are continuous systems that move water and nutrients from roots to leaves and from leaves to roots. Water and nutrients are absorbed by the tiniest root hairs and moved by the xylem – very quickly, I might add – to the very tips of your leaves. Without water, our leaves wilt and die."

Xylem moves water and nutrients UP from roots to leaves

Phloem moves glucose DOWN from leaves to roots

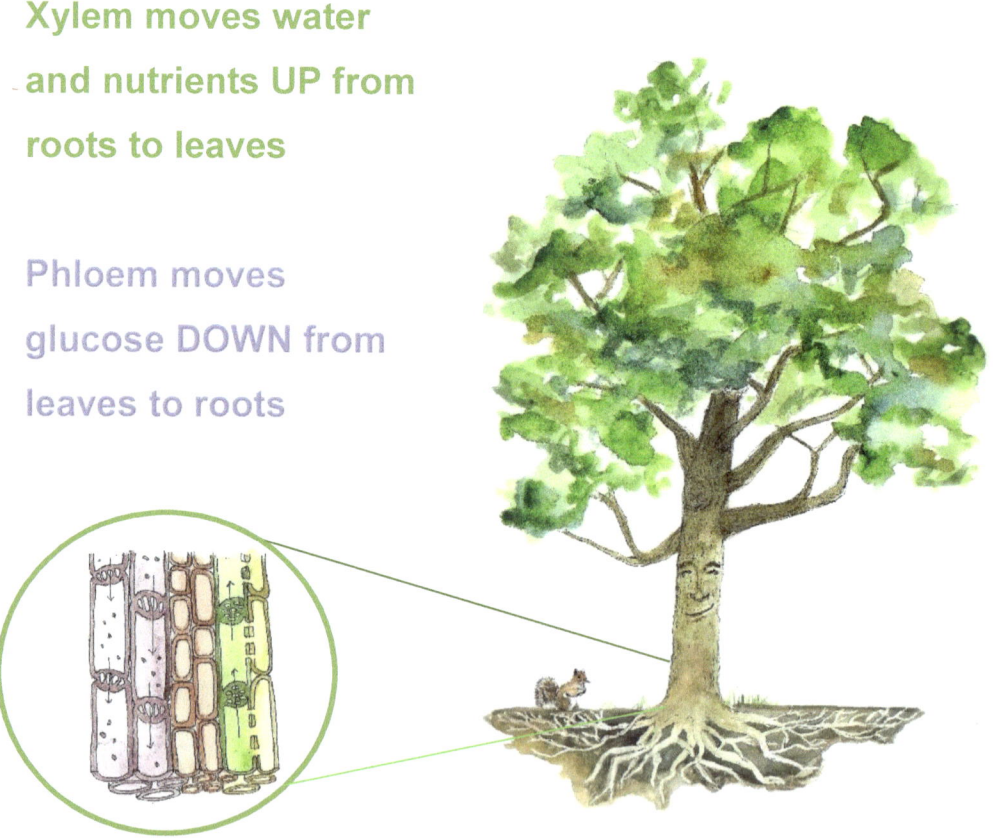

"What about the nutrients?" A question popped up near my feet. I looked down and there stood my three friends.

"I thought you had gone to hear someone else," I quizzed.

"We decided it's no fun without you," Stormy replied with a grin.

"Excuse me!" Chloe interrupted, "Is there a question or are you holding your own seminar!"

"We're sorry! Yes, there was a question," I slumped to the ground as Stormy repeated his question. "What about the nutrients? You said without water, the leaves would die. What do the nutrients do?" "A fine question! You didn't let that one pass you by," Chloe answered proudly.

I have noticed that the aged trees are particularly happy and proud when the young ones are inquisitive. I scratched a careful note for my report.

"Nutrients are essential, too. Do you know how many there are?" Chloe inquired while looking around at many sad faces. All eyes were evading Chloe's gaze. "I'm surprised and astounded!!" said Chloe. She swayed back and forth at the front of the crowd, her huge canopy shaking sadly side to side. Moments passed eternally! Quiet was interrupted by a quartet of trees moving from the crowd and merging to the front. Everyone in the crowd looked at each other with great expressions of wonder.

"HMM. HMMM. HMMMMM. HMMMMMMM."

"Nitrogen, potassium, phosphorus,

Macro-nutrients important to us.

But don't forget calcium, sulfur, and zinc.

Without them we would surely sink.

Magnesium, manganese, boron, too,

Keep us growing gracefully through

Dry times and wet times and all in-betweens.

Micro-nutrients great -- If you know what we mean.

Copper and chlorine round out the pack

Of nutrients we do not wish to lack.

Oh, oh one is left. We forgot to bring

Mol-yb-de-num -- hard to say and harder to sing!"

Cheering erupted!! I had to admit that was quite a song and excellent harmony. The quartet bowed and bowed; I thought they would surely crack. Meanwhile Chloe stood to the side glowing. The four singers retreated to their respective places amongst the pleased crowd. Branches, twigs, and leaves patted them as they strode past. What a fun place! I looked at Stormy, Internode, and Thorny. They were jiggling with delight. It took a few moments, but Chloe was able to begin anew.

"Now those are the nutrients!" she said.

"But what do they do?" questioned a larger sapling off to my left.

"Everything!!" boomed Chloe. "All those nutrients are needed by our cells so we grow taller, broader and healthier."

Thorny held in his breath to puff out his trunk. Internode and Stormy snickered.

Chloe continued, "*Transpiration*, *photosynthesis*, seed and fruit formation, root growth, leaf drop, and wound closure, are just a few of the functions of these incredible nutrients. All the processes that keep you alive are made possible by them."

"Wow!" gasped the audience. Cheers erupted!

"We get most of them from the soil, but a small portion is taken in by our leaves." Chloe continued.

"Do we, or I mean, you, always have enough?" I stammered and felt my cheeks redden.

"Our human friend is feeling like one of us!" Chloe laughed with the crowd. "Actually there can be a problem on either side. If we get too much or too little of one nutrient, it influences another nutrient which in turn affects all of our processes. It's a delicate balance. A harmonious balance, if you know what I mean!" Chloe smiled and gestured to our quartet.

"Enough of the *xylem*," she continued. "No! Wait! I forgot something important. How could I have done that? My, my – I must be getting old."

"Maybe you need an extra nutrient!" one of the older burs in the crowd teased.

Chloe moved on with a wry smile cracking her bark.

"The *xylem* – some is alive, but most is dead!"

Gasps roamed their way around the crowd, while everyone looked at themselves carefully.

"I don't feel dead," responded an older bur.

"I know," said Chloe, "and you shouldn't feel that way, for the dead *xylem* tissue is most vital. Human, come to the front, please," Chloe asked.

I immediately looked around me and everyone laughed. Of course, Chloe meant me. I was the only human in the grove. Trees patted me on the head as I nervously worked my way through to the front. Little squirrels jumped from tree to tree watching my progress. They were curious as to my being summoned to the front. So was I.

"Human," Chloe began, "What keeps you standing?"

"I don't know; I guess my legs," I stated with reservation.

"That's partly true," remarked Chloe, "But what else?"

I began to realize Chloe was trying to make a connection between what's inside me that helps me stand and what makes trees stand.

"Oh," I said with sudden realization, "my skeleton keeps me standing!"

"That's correct. And for trees to stand upright there must be something inside as well. The dead *xylem* tissue keeps us standing."

I remembered that the insides of trees are used by humans for lumber, but I decided not to mention it. It didn't seem an appropriate bit of information. A tiny wiggling branch could be seen toward the back of the group. I recognized it as Internode. "Chloe," I said, "I believe someone is trying to get your attention."

Chloe peered to the back and signaled for Internode to come ahead. Flanked by my other two friends, they reluctantly moved forward. I chuckled for they bunched together so tightly they looked like a bush striding forward with someone hiding inside. Others chuckled too, watching the procession. Finally they made their entrance.

Chloe waited and at length asked, "Did you have a question or were you cooling off your leaves?"

Thorny stammered, "If the dead *xylem* helps us stand up, what does the living *xylem* do?"

"Splendid question!" Chloe beamed. "Can anyone tell us?"

With that the "three-as-one" shuffled quickly to me. I sat cross-legged on the ground at the front of the crowd expecting the answer momentarily as Thorny, Internode, and Stormy tried to sit on my lap. The jostling and giggling caused a raised eyebrow and downward glance from Chloe.

"You DO want to hear the answer DON'T you?"

We immediately ceased our revelry with silence! And more silence!

"Well," said Chloe, "it appears some are lacking in their education. But that's WHY we are here!!"

Chloe seemed tickled at the prospect, and then began, "If we have a good year, lots of rain, good soil, much warmth, etc., etc., etc.!..."Lots of nutrients flow through the *xylem*, racing from the roots to our branches and our leaves," continued Chloe. "Ohhh! It is superb. We are well-supplied with our needs. But, what would happen if we had too much? "

I grinned; I know what happened to Uncle Charlie. He got fat. "You store it in the *xylem*!!" I yelled with such force that I lost my lap friends. Then I was embarrassed! "Sorry," I said.

Chloe rocked back and began to shake. I actually saw tears streak down her bark. Then a huge laugh erupted from deep inside her. It became infectious. Everyone joined in and slowly, I chuckled along. I guess my revelation surprised everyone – even me.

Once re-gaining control, Chloe stated, "Yes, that is exactly it. There are special cells in the living *xylem* that store nutrients for later use. Not every year is a good one, so when we are able, we store up for the future, much like our friend, the squirrel." Chloe pointed overhead.

I remembered Aesop's fable of "The ant and the grasshopper". The ant stored food for later times, but the grasshopper didn't. Then I thought of my savings account. Hmmm. Make a note to check it when I return home.

"Now that is the *xylem*. What do you think the *phloem* does?" questioned Chloe. "I'll give you a hint. Remember, the *xylem* moves water and nutrients from the soil to the leaves."

"OOOOO!" A young sapling to our left was jumping up and down madly waving branches.

"I believe someone wants to answer," Chloe smiled at the group. "Go ahead!"

"Well, I think," started the sapling, "if the *xylem* goes up, something has to come down."

"Good thinking, young one! Next question: what comes down in the *phloem*?"

"Hmmm," the young sapling's face twisted with considerable thought. It looked from its base to its canopy and then back. And then it began the process again. "I know!! If the *xylem* moves water and nutrients from the roots to the leaves, the leaves must send something back to the roots!!!"

"Ahhh!! Exactly!!" Chloe stretched with pride. "When the sun hits your leaves and mixes with water and carbon dioxide - thanks to our human," Chloe bowed toward me, "carbohydrate energy is produced. This energy flows downward in the *phloem* and is deposited throughout our branches and roots. Without this process, our roots won't grow."

"Remember," she went on, "the dead *xylem* is deep inside us, but the living *xylem* and *phloem* are very near the surface, right under our bark. This is very important to remember! Damage to our bark, even very slight, has severe consequences to our system." Chloe's gaze was directed toward the front row. I could be wrong, but I swear Chloe was looking directly at me. I glanced from side to side and realized they were all looking at me. Even my little pals were eyeing me strangely. I couldn't help it, I blurted out, "Did I do something?"

Chloe leaned toward me and said with an ominous hush, "It will be revealed to you in time!"

"HMMMMM! HMMMMMMMMM!!! HMMMMMMMMMMMMM!! HMMMMMMMMMMMM!" Humming and swaying began, as the quartet entered front stage. The quartet began to sing for it signaled the end of Chloe's time.

"*Xylem* and *phloem*

It all began

Running top to bottom

And back again.

Carrying water,

Nutrients, and en-er-gy

Important parts of me – a Tree!"

The crowd dispersed repeating, "*Xylem* and *Phloem*........."

I picked myself up from the ground, stretched and sang, "*Xylem* and *Phloem*, da da, da, da. Where shall we go now, gang?"

Waving branches assured me that they were directing me to hear another adventurous story. I followed.

Chapter 8 - Flo's Hospital Zone

Sobs, sniffles and sighs seemed out of place amidst the singing surrounding Chloe's tales. But I was sure I heard them. I shifted my body to get a fix on the sounds. There they were again! More muffled sobs. Steering in the direction of the ever increasing murmurs and pain-filled wails, I spotted a sparse group of burs along the outer edge. Creeping closer, my pals and I listened intently. A soothing voice among the sobs came from a short but very wide bur who talked like a nurse. "It looks terrible, love! What happened?" A tender branch gently folded itself around the trunk of the sad, sniffling tree.

"I was growing strong and healthy," explained the sad sniffling tree, "shading the house with great pride and joy. One day the man and two little ones ran outside. The man carried something. I couldn't tell what it was. Suddenly, I was whacked on this lower branch. OHHH! OHHH!" The tree sobbed, pointing to a thin and deformed branch.

"There, there, love!" stated Nurse Flo. "Let it out! Continue whenever you want." A giant branch gave a slight pat and tug of embrace to the wailing tree. Sniffles and wheezes were all that could be heard for several minutes. It was during this pause, I realized this solemn and reflective group was listening intently to every word. The other thing I noticed was their saddened, furrowed bark faces, ragged parts, broken branches, stripped and torn bark, and strange canopies. They looked like casualties crowding a hospital tent in the aftermath of a war. My thoughts were drawn back to the object of our attention as the sobbing died down to a few shudders.

"They were all laughing," the sobbing tree resumed her story, "and I actually loved their joy when a long, narrow vine-looking item gripped tightly around the bark on my branch. The other end of the long thing appeared on my limb two feet from the first vine-like thing. The man cinched them tightly around my branch and formed a "U" shape just above the ground. He placed something in-between at the bottom of the "U" -- such a curious ritual, I thought. Next, one of the little ones sat on the item, the man pushed her and it began to swing back and forth. It didn't hurt much that year, and they were having such fun, I didn't even pay attention. But I did notice my leaves at the end of that branch yellowed earlier than the rest of my leaves and then fell off long before autumn."

"The following year my leaves were worse," continued the sobbing bur, "As I grew, the rope tightened on my bark. Each year after that, my branch growth decreased because, my *xylem* and *phloem* had been cut off. No *carbohydrates* moved from my leaves and nothing came from my roots to the leaves. I was a mess; my branch was starving." Groans and gasps resounded from the gathering. A few more sniffles flowed from the patient before he continued the sad tale. "Yes, my branch could no longer receive water and nutrients from my roots. The leaves didn't come back and the branch died!" With this, the bur completely broke down. But the silent shaking of the tree was far worse than the wailing. It was a sign of resignation that a once beautiful, strong healthy branch was gone. The bur slowly lumbered away, shaking still.

An eerie quiet descended over the group like fog covering a beautiful valley meadow. Within moments, tales of horror and emotion rolled from the audience like an avalanche of snow billowing from the blue sky above the jagged Sierra Nevada Mountains. One yellow-leafed, weak-voiced bur told of dogs being chained around her trunk for several years. "The endless barking and circling my trunk with the chain girdled me and drastically reduced my nutrients and carbohydrate flow by cutting through the *xylem* and *phloem*," she explained with great sadness.

Another broke in among the responding wails to explain his unnatural-looking canopy. "For decades, I grew majestically in hopes of being a national champion tree. Then new people moved into my home. I thought I was developing beautifully. I stretched with pride when they came outside to admire me. To my horror, they were not happy with me. I heard my people and another man say things like, "Too Big! Branches will fall on the roof! Too Old! Probably over-mature." OVER MATURE!! The nerve!! I am ….or WAS in my prime."

She continued to describe her disgrace when the man with a chainsaw and a truck finished his deed. "In one sweep of the man's buzzing, outstretched arm, a branch on my left fell and then another, and another were lopped off. Haphazard hacking at my canopy produced the hideous result you see before you. I nearly didn't attend our gathering for fear of being ridiculed for my ugliness."

A soulful, whispered wail swayed like a breeze across a prairie marsh. It reached a crescendo that was frightening. I felt an increasing awkwardness, as I did with the earlier pencil and paper episode, but this time I couldn't fix it. Apparently, we, humans, do so much damage. I felt a heavy burden to right this wrong. Before I could think of sealing my ideas of correction on paper, a young grotesque-looking sapling arose to speak.

"Love? UH, what is it good for? Nothing! Absolutely Nothing!"

The phrase was vaguely familiar, I mused. But before I could place it, he spoke.

"Since I'm young, my bark has not developed its tough, corky layers. This makes me a prime target for creative **'Lovers' ",** he stated in a mocking tone.

"Couple after couple traipses through my woods, listening for snorting bucks. Not content with that, however, they settle themselves at the base of my trunk, cooing and cuddling, which leads to … **CARVING**!! Yes, carving their undying love in my precious, thin bark."

Wails gushed forth like the removal of your thumb from a leaking dam. Their compassionate, rhythmic wailing brought chills to my body and salty tears to my eyes. I was moved!

"Cutting into my bark, especially when it's thin and tender, causes the same problems that girdling my trunk or branch would. The worst part is that nothing happens quickly. "Wouldn't that be funny," he said with a smirk. "If THEY damaged us and we immediately died. Like fell in their laps!"

Bouts of raucous laughter bounded across the crowd as the injured group pictured the response to their demise after being damaged by humans. I had to laugh myself, but I did wonder what prevents the tree from dying right away. Someone was obviously reading my brain waves for the next voice asked just that.

"Why don't we die immediately when we're damaged?" asked a soft voice next to my leg. I looked down to see my buddies with Stormy's branch held high. Dear Flo had been standing quietly to the side, listening intently, but now began.

"Ah, my sweet loves! You have suffered greatly and I'm truly saddened by these troubles! The answer to that question has to do with the way we are gloriously made. Remember what Chloe said about reserves?" Several branches waved slowly.

I nodded with intensity and gathered Stormy, Internode, and Thorny close around me. I did remember. This is what Chloe meant about me finding out about damaging the *phloem* and *xylem*. Suddenly I felt so angry, the things human's do.

"In good years, we store up reserves in our *xylem*," continued Flo. "Then when damage occurs, we use the reserves to protect ourselves. If damage occurs over and over and over, we can't store enough reserves and we weaken and eventually die."

I jumped up, knocking my pals over. "I'm sorry, I'm sorry. I'll do what I can to stop these terrible things from happening to you!" Flo lumbered over to me and with her entire canopy embraced me. Thorny, Internode, and Stormy wrapped themselves around my legs. After some time, I moved away from Flo and headed away from the crowd. I could see wet stains flowing down their furrowed bark. I kept repeating, "I'm sorry, I'm sorry."

I needed to move on to think about what I had just experienced. As I plodded away, I heard strange noises, strange, because they were the sounds of laughter. I tried to walk away from the happiness, but I was drawn toward it.

Chapter 9 -Beginnings

I recognized the laughter now as the happy, chortling sounds of OOOHs and AAAHs.

"OH, isn't that the sweetest thing you've ever seen," cooed a young sapling.

"I don't think it was here yesterday. W-when do you suppose it broke through the ground?" questioned a larger bur.

"We must be careful to protect it," another bur added excitedly.

"Humph, ground-rats, moss sweepers!" grumped an ageing oak behind me.

Ignoring the ageing oak, a young sapling pointed to the ground and squeaked, "How did it get there, Darla?"

A branch carefully and gently wrapped around the curious extended twig and Darla began, "It's a miracle, Da-a-rling. Let me explain."

I worked my way toward the focus of their attention.

"Watch out!" shrieked a few voices. I stopped in mid-step and realized I was about to tread on a green spot nearly hidden amid the bare soil. From my vantage point, that's all it looked like. Then it began to squirm and move from side to side. I dropped to all fours, my pals scrambling with me. I smiled up and said, "Thanks for the warning!" I saw two leaves, very small, but they were definitely bur oak. I was beginning to recognize them now. I remembered Lobelia's leaf tales.

Darla settled the gathering into a small, informal circle around this tiny miracle in the soil. Darla, I learned, was from the southern range, which I suspected, for her drawl had that soothing, magical melody I had heard while I was covering the southern route of the Presidential primary in Tennessee.

I sat on the ground and leaned back against Charlie, a large bur. Getting comfortable, I glanced up to see a pleasant smile crack on his thick bark. With a little wink, he brushed the air with his giant branch and a cool breeze blew across my face. It was very soothing awaiting the upcoming wonderful story. I wasn't surprised in the next instant to see Stormy wriggling through the crowd and curling up into my lap, much like my dog Maxx. It felt good and homey. I closed my eyes for an instant, thinking that Maxx would be having a grand time with all these trees. I chuckled at the thought.

Darla's pleasing drawl permeated the air. "How did this dainty, precious, two-leaf seedling arrived at such a grand time in our history - you wonder??" she chuckled.

"The beautiful flower is where it begins."

Slowly, golden-yellow, curly, whiffs floated through the air above us.

"What's that?" shouted excited onlookers.

"Show off!" blurted my neighbor.

I was confused about all this yellow stuff. On another assignment in North Carolina, I had seen a similar yellow, powdery substance dropping in layers all over yards, houses, and cars. I never found out what it was.

"Da-a-arlings!" said Darla. "Don't be alarmed. It's a special time and it happens to all of us. Without it, our generations would not continue. What you see suspended above you is pollen, thousands, maybe millions of very fine grains of pollen. It comes from those male flowers or *catkins* that Joseph spoke about."

"How does it get out here?" asked Thorny.

"Foo, Foo, Fooooo," repeated Darla. "Do what I do everyone. Foo, Foo, Fooooo," she continued.

Quizzical faces turned side-to-side, each searching for an answer.

"I believe she's gone daffy!" chortled one bur behind me.

Darla encouraged us all and slowly, "Foo, Foo, Fooooo's", began erupting across the audience. Once we got used to it, it was fun, but I still didn't understand why.

"Look, the yellow sky is moving!" shouted an excited young bur.

"Excellent!" exclaimed Darla.

"What ARE we doing?" I asked. "And what is the purpose of this pollen in nature? Don't new oak trees sprout when squirrels bury acorns and forget about them? What do these millions of particles of oak pollen dust do for oak trees or any newly-sprouted oak seedlings?"

"OHHHH! DAAARLING, DAAAARLING! How sweet of you to ask?" Darla responded. "You are Ab-So-Lute-Ly correct about the acorns. When squirrels bury them, new oak trees sprout." As if on cue, two squirrels raced up a large tree near the front and jumped from branch to branch, and tree to tree, finally flinging themselves to the ground behind me. Twitters of giggles bounced with them as each tree responded to their tiny feet and tails rustling through the limbs.

"How charming!!" quipped Darla. "But where was I? Oh yes, pollen! The wonderful thing about nature is that without the pollen, no acorns. No acorns means, no more trees. This tiny young one that you see before you would not be here and our species would quickly evaporate." Sad faces and crinkling of bark were evident as the group pondered that possibility. "Ah, but don't fear. The process continues", Darla mused as she bent down to look at the tiny seedling. Her pause lingered for a long time.

Finally Stormy spoke up. "Well, what is it called and how does it happen?"

"Oh, you want to know more?" Darla said glowing..

Cheers of agreement were heard from every corner.

"Well," she began as she sauntered across the front and whisked her giant branches from side to side, like a southern belle promenading in the parlor.

"Pollination is what happens. Every tree has flowers, even if you can't see them. Ours ARE very small."

Much rustling was heard as trees began to explore themselves.

"Ooh, Ooh, Ooh!! I think I found one," an excited youngster pointed at an elder bur to its right, "It's drooping. Is it dead?"

"NO, NO!" Darla responded with pleasure. "I will explain. Some trees have perfect flowers, meaning that both male, called *staminate*, and female called *pistillate* parts are in the same flower. We BURS, however, have imperfect flowers. There are both male and female flowers on the same tree, but on different parts of the tree. The droopy grouping of flowers is the staminate flowers and it is called a *catkin*. The female flower eventually becomes the acorn."

"Imperfect!" grumped an old tree. "Why I never heard such rubbish. I am quite perfect!!"

Darla, overhearing the comment, explained, "Imperfect is just a way of explaining that burs have two types of flowers, male and female, on the same tree. You know, we need both flowers to produce acorns. It is still a perfect system."

"I knew I would like this talk!" Stormy chuckled while tickling me in the rib with his tiny limb.

I laughed, "Yes, it sounds like the birds and bees to me."

Darla shot a look our way and we tried to shrink out of sight.

"As I was saying, and I know Joseph talked of this, some trees have only male flowers or only female flowers. Our cousins, ginkgo, ash, and holly, are like this. They are *dioecious*, which means 'two houses'. It takes two trees for fruit to form. And only the tree with the female flowers produces the fruit.

"Isn't nature MARRRVELOUS!!" sang Darla. "AHHHHHH!"

"Back to us, and our brother and sister oaks, we are *monecious*, as Joseph mentioned, is a fancy word for 'one house'. We have male and female flowers on the same tree. It doesn't take two trees to produce an acorn. The staminate, or male flowers as I mentioned before, produce pollen which then lands onto the female flower."

"Wow, I can't wait till I can do that!" shouted Stormy. "But why were we making all that noise earlier, all that Foo Fooo stuff?"

"Perfect question, little one! You will become a storyteller someday, I just know it!"

Stormy puffed his branches and settled in for more answers.

"The wind moves the pollen from one oak tree to another," Darla continued. That's why we produce enormous amounts of pollen. It's critical to producing future bur oaks that are strong and long-lived. The pollen finds a female flower and the acorn begins. Without the pollen and the wind, the acorn would not exist."

About then, something hard hit my head. I thought it was one of my friends playing another joke, but then I saw the object roll around at my feet. I bent down to pick it up and another hit my back. I looked up to see more of these round objects hanging from one of the elder burs right over my head. That's when I noticed the chuckling and shaking of his limbs.

"Very funny," I stated. "What are these?"

"Acorns, darling!" Darla stated. "Baby oaks at your fingertips."

I examined the acorn with my reporter's eyes. It was quite large, nearly covering my palm. There was a top and a bottom. An elder bur next to me said, "The top is called a *cap*, and it covers the top the acorn. Did you attend Cork's talk about buds?" she questioned.

"Yes, I did, but what has that to do with acorns?"

"Take a good look at the cap," she stated.

"Hey, there are lots of hairy projections on the acorn cap. They look like the projections on the *terminal* bud." I said. I also noticed that the cap was real bumpy.

"It's one of the largest acorns in the oak family," she informed me.

"Oh, oh, something's happening." Darla moved away from our group to join other massive oaks passing behind us. I sensed our time here was complete. Movement was beginning at every corner of the grove.

"What's happening, Darla?" I asked as my three friends stayed close to my legs.

She motioned for us to follow a line that was forming beside a small patch of trees. Darla waited for me and pointed toward the edge of the forest patch. "Another beginning," she stated. "See the log on the ground?"

I nodded, but was unsure what was meant by a beginning. All I could see was a rotting log. I wondered why the owner of the forest hadn't cleaned up the mess. "What do you mean 'beginning'? My grandfather would have moved that old log out of the woods long time ago."

"Many humans are unaware of the importance of a fallen tree," Darla explained. "It fulfills an important mission. Our death brings life to the forest.

Nutrients remain in us and when we die, we become a fertile field for new trees – a beginning. Look closely; you young ones, too!"

My friends and I knelt close to the fallen log. That's when I noticed the solemnity of the passing line of burs. As they passed this log and others, they lowered their canopies. I heard Thorny, Stormy, and Internode with hushed voices murmuring amongst themselves. "It ends and begins here," they said. I was understanding, and without thinking reached out for the bits and pieces of the log. Gasps wafted from the burs behind me. Darla quickly calmed everyone. "It's all right. It's the only way for the human to learn."

I looked toward Darla as she nodded, "Go ahead. What do you feel?"
I picked up the dark, cool fragments below the log. "Soil!" I exclaimed. "The log has turned to soil." I examined the soil closely and continued to move items around. I spotted lots of little wiggling and crawling creatures, mushrooms, and then I spotted it. Another tiny bur with its roots firmly planted in the newly-made soil.

"It's the end and then the beginning. A circle of life," Darla stated as she laid a branch on my shoulder. I rose up to see Papa Root, Lobelia, Joseph, Flo, Chloe and Ashley Oak beaming and waving as they lumbered off in various directions.

"Where are they going?" I asked.

"Dispersing throughout our range, going back for another year to spread our story to all who will listen," Darla stated as she moved south with another small group of burs.

"But, I have so much to learn."

"Next year! Come back!" Ashley called as she headed east.

I looked down at my friends. Tears ran through their little bark fissures. I was full of new knowledge and ready to report, but I felt empty knowing we were dispersing. I sat on the ground and opened my lap for my tiny little friends. We leaned against the log with Internode fanning me with his tiny oak leaves. I closed my eyes and felt the cool breeze. A tear trickled down my cheek, and I squeezed my friends closer. The breezes grew faster and my tears flowed.

"Hey, hey, are you all right?" a voice from the past shouted. "Wake up! You're going to get soaked. Where are you from? Don't you know when to come in out of the rain?" he snickered. I looked up to see someone in a uniform. It was the ranger who gave me directions to Bur Oak. I blinked, jumped up, and looked all around.

"Where did they go?" I asked.

"Who? I didn't see anyone when I drove up. Are you sure you're OK? Did you fall and hit your head?"

"I – I, yes, I'm all right. I was looking for Bur Oak."

The ranger laughed and headed for his green truck. "I think you found it as he pointed to a small twig lodged between my windshield wiper and the window. As I stumbled toward the door of my jeep, I saw the *obtuse, tawny* twig with hairy projections surrounding the clustered *terminal* buds.

"I DO think you found it, "he chuckled."

I tucked the twig in my pocket and glanced around the horizon to see small dust cyclones forming in every direction.

I turned back to find the ranger and his green truck gone.

Glossary Terms

Abscission is the normal separation of a leaf, fruit, or flower from a plant. Abscissic acid is the plant hormone involved in abscission. (1) *Word origin is early 15th C Latin for removal or cutting off.* (5)

Annual rings are concentric circles that appear on tree trunk cross-sections that mark the end of a growing season. These rings show whether the tree grew a lot or a little that year. Also called tree rings or growth rings. (1) *Its origin is 1875-80. (5)*

Axil of a plant is the angle between the upper side of the stem and a leaf, branch, or petiole. In flowering plants, the bud develops in the axil of a leaf. (1) *Word origin is Latin for armpit 1785 – 95. (5)*

Bark is the outer covering of the trunk, branches, and roots of trees. (1) *Word origin is before 900; Middle English berken, ld English beorcan; akin to Old to Old English borcian to bark, Old Norse berdja to bluseer, Lithuanian burgeti to growl, quarrel, Serbo-Croatian brgljats to murmur. (5)*

Branching – *Word origin is 1250-1300, Middle English, bra(u)nche, Anglo French; Old French branche , Late Lantin branca paw, of uncertain origin. (5)*

> Alternate branching of leaves or buds is a pattern in which there is one leaf (or bud) per node, and one on the opposite side of the stem but not in pairs. (1) *Word origin for alternate is 1635-1645 Latin altern – interchangeable, alternating, equivalent. (5)*

> Opposite branching of leaves or buds is a pattern in which there is one leaf (or bud) per node on one side of a branch with another leaf directly opposite as in pairs. (1) *Word origin for oppose is 1350-1400 Middle English, Old French oppose, blend of Latin opponere meaning to set against and Old French poser. (5)*

Bud is a small, developing part of a plant that will grow into a flower, a new leaf or a stem. (1) *Word origin occurs between 1350-1400, Middle English budde bud, spray, pod; akin to German Hagebutte - hip, Old Norse budda –purse; dialectal Swedish bodd –head; Dutch buidel - bag, purse; Middle Low German guddich – swollen. (5)*

> Adventitious buds grow from an unusual part of the tree. (1) *Word origin is from 1595-1605; Latin adventicius literally, coming from without, external, equivalent to. (5)*

> Axillary buds grow from the axil area of the leaf between petiole and branch. (1) *Word origin from 1605-1615 is Latin for armpit. (5)*

> Dormant buds grow in response to different environmental or biological conditions (like droughts, cold seasons or wounding) (1). *Word origin is 1350-*

1400; Middle English dorma; Anglo French dormer, Latin to sleep. (5)

Lateral buds are on the side of the branch. (1) *Word origin is from 1590-1600; Latin lateralis of the side, equivalent to later – (stem of latus) side +alis. (5)*

Terminal buds grow at the end of a branch or stem. (5) *Word origin is from 1480-90; late Middle English, Latin terminalis, equivalent to termin(us) – end. (5)*

Bud scale is a modified leaf (or similar structure) that covers and protects the bud. (1) *The term bud scale was first used in 1875-1880. The term scale originated in 1250-1300, Middle English; Middle French – escale; West Germanic – skala, ak in to scale; late Middle English – scalen to removes scales from. (5)*

Bud scale scar is what remains on the branch after the scale has fallen off. The bud scale scars are unique to different species of trees and help to identify one from another. (5) *Word origin for scar occurred around 1350-1400; Middle English; aphetic variant of eschar. (5)*

Callus tissue - undifferentiated tissue formed by the cambium, usually as the result of wounding (contrast with woundwood). (1) *Word origin for callus began around 1375-1425; late Middle English Latin callosus – hard skinned, tough, equivalent to call (um) tough skin, any hard substance. Word origin for tissue was around 1325-75; Middle English tissew, variant of tissue; Middle French, Old French, noun use of past participle of tistre to weave; Latin texere . (5)*

Carbohydrates are a large class of organic compounds consisting of carbon, hydrogen, and oxygen, usually with twice as many hydrogen atoms as carbon or oxygen atoms. Carbohydrates are produced in green plants by photosynthesis. Sugars, starches, and cellulose are all carbohydrates. (2) *Word origin is 1865-70; carbo- form meaning "Carbon," abstracted 1810 from carbon + hydrate which occurred around 1795-1805 from hydr-+ -ate (Time for you to look this one up!) (5)*

Chlorophyll is a molecule that uses light energy from sunlight to turn water and carbon dioxide gas into sugar and oxygen (this process is called photosynthesis). Chlorophyll is magnesium based and is usually green. (1) *Word origin 1810-20; chloro+ -phyll; (Another to look up, I can't give you everything.) (5)*

Chloroplast are small green structures in plants that contain chlorophyll. Leaves have many chloroplasts. (1) *Word origin is from 1885-90; chloro(phyll) (from above discovery) + -plast from Greek plastós formed, molded, equivalent to plath-, base of plássein to form, mold + -tos verbal adjective suffix, with tht. (5)*

Cuneate means wedge-shaped. (1) *Origin is from 1800-10; Latin cuneātus, equivalent to cuneā (re) to wedge, secure by wedging, become wedge-shaped + -tus past participle suffix; see –ate. (5)*

Deciduous plants lose their leaves seasonally, usually for the dry season. Some deciduous plants include ash, beech, hickory, maple, and oak. (1) *Word origin occurs between 1650-60; Latin dēciduus tending to fall, falling, equivalent to dēcid (ere) to fall off, down (dē- de- + -cidere, combining form of cadere to fall) + -uus deverbal adj. suffix; see –ous. (5)*

Decomposers are organisms like fungi and certain bacteria that break down and digest the remains of organisms. (1) *Word originates from a combination of de or dis Latin (akin to bis, Greek dís twice); before f, dif-; before some consonants, di-; often replacing obsolete des- < Old French; com Latin, variant of preposition cum with; pose is from 1325-75; (v.) Middle English posen < Middle French poser < Late Latin pausāre to stop, cease, rest, derivative of Latin pausa pause; French poser has taken over the basic sense of Latin pōnere "to put, place" and represents it in French borrowings of its prefixed derivatives (see compose, depose, etc.), probably reinforced by the accidental resemblance of poser to. Wow! Complicated is language!! (5)*

Decomposition is the decay or breakdown of things into more basic elements. For example, after a plant dies, it decomposes into organic nutrients. (1) *Check origin of the ending.*

Dioecious is Greek for "two households" meaning one plant has male (staminate) flowers and another plant has female or (pistillate) flowers on another plant. (6) Examples are maple, ash, ginkgo. (Compare with monoecious.) *Word origin is from 1740-50; New Latin Dioeci (a) a class name (di- di-+ Greek oikía a house, dwelling, spelling variant of oîkos) + -ous. (5)*

Earlywood (early wood or springwood) is the part of the wood in a growth ring of a tree that is produced early in the growing season. The cells are larger and have thinner walls than those produced later in the growing season. (2) *Word origin is from 1910-15. (5)*

Fungus (plural fungi) are organisms that obtain energy by breaking down dead organic material and that produce spores. Some fungi include mushrooms, toadstools, slime molds, yeast, penicillium mold, and mildew. Classification: kingdom Fungus. (1) *Word origin is from 1520-30; Latin: fungus, mushroom; perhaps akin to Greek spóngos, sphóngos sponge. (5)*

Hyphae (singular hypha) are any of the filaments that constitute the body (mycelium) of a fungus. (1) *Origin occurs from 1865-70 from Greek meaning web. (5)*

Internode the part of a plant stem between nodes (1). *Word origin is from 1660-70 from Latin internodium – inter (between) and node (knot) from Latin 1565-75. (5)*

Latewood (late wood or summerwood) is the part of the wood in a growth ring of a tree that is produced later in the growing season. The cells of late wood are smaller and have thicker cell walls than those produced earlier in the season. Within a growth ring, the change of early wood to late wood is gradual, but each layer of early wood from the next growing season makes an abrupt contrast with the late wood before it, thus leading to the perception of rings. (2) *Word origin is from 1925-30. (5)*

A <u>leaf</u> is an outgrowth of a <u>plant</u> that grows from a node in the stem. Most leaves are flat and contain chloroplasts; their main function is to make food energy through photosynthesis. The first leaf to grow from a seed is called the <u>cotyledon</u>.(1) *Word origin is before 900; Middle English leef, lef, Old English lēaf; cognate with Dutch loof, German Laub, Old Norse lauf, Gothic laufs. (5)*

A <u>lobed</u> <u>leaf</u> is one in which the margin is divided into rounded or pointed sections and the incisions (cuts) go less than halfway to the midrib. (1) *Word originates from 1515-25; Medieval Latin lobus (Late Latin: hull, husk, pod); Greek lobós, akin to Latin legula lobe of the ear. (5)*

<u>Margins</u> of a leaf are its edges, which vary from plant to plant. The margins can be smooth, serrated, or toothed; they can also be lobed or entire. (1) *Word originates from 1300-50; Middle English; Latin margin- (stem of margō) border; akin to march. (5)*

<u>Monecious</u> plants have the male (pistillate) and female (staminate) reproductive organs on the same plant, such as oaks. (1) *Word origin is 18 century from New Latin monoecia, from mono- (meaning one) + Greek oikos house. (5)*

<u>Mushrooms</u> are fast-growing fungi (they are not plants). They grow in dark, damp places and reproduce via spores. (1) *Word origin is from 1350-1400; alteration (by folk etymology) of Middle English muscheron, musseroun; Middle French mousseron; Late Latin mussiriōn-, stem of mussiriō. Now you can look up the origin of those other words. (5)*

<u>Mycorrhiza</u> is a fungus that grows in a symbiotic relationship with the roots (or rhizoids) of a plant. (1) *Word origin is from 1890-95; myco- + -rrhiza. Another compound word for you to look up. (5)*

A <u>node</u> is the point on a stem where a leaf is attached or has been attached; a joint. (2) *Word originates from 1565-75; and is Latin nōdus for knot. (5)*

A <u>nutrient</u> is a chemical that an organism need to ingest in order to survive (like fats, carbohydrates, vitamins, minerals, etc.). (1) *Word origin is 1640-50; Latin nūtrient- (stem of nūtriēns), present participle of nūtrīre to feed, nourish; see —ent. (5)*

<u>Obovate</u> is a leaf or similar flat part shaped like the longitudinal section of an egg with the narrower end at the base; inversely ovate. (3) *Word origin is 1775-85; ob- a prefix meaning "toward," "to," "on," "over," "against," originally occurring in loanwords from Latin, but now used also, with the sense of "reversely," "inversely," to form Neo-Latin and English scientific terms: object; obligate; oblanceolate.+ ovate meaning from 1750-60; Latin ōvātus, equivalent to ōv (um) egg+ -ātus —ate. (5)*

Obtuse is a blunt or rounded at the apex, the converging edges separated by an angle greater than 90 degrees. (4) *Interesting origin and history of the term - Early 15c., "dull, blunted," from Middle French obtus (fem. obtuse), from Latin obtusus "blunted, dull," also used figuratively, past participle of obtundere "to beat against, make dull," from ob "against" (see ob-) + tundere "to beat," from PIE *(s)tud-e- "to beat, strike, push, thrust," from root *(s)teu- "to push, stick, knock, beat" (cf. Latin tudes "hammer," Sanskrit tudati "he thrusts"). Sense of "stupid" is first found c.1500. Related: Obtusely; obtuseness. Which do you think is associated with our term?*

An organelle is a membrane-bound structure within a plant's cell (and all eukaryotic cells) where specialized metabolic tasks occur. Some organelles include the nucleus, nucleolus, mitochondria, the ER (endoplamic reticulum), and lysosomes. (1) *Word origin is 1905-10; New Latin organella, diminutive of Latin organum organ; see —elle. (5)*

A perfect flower has both male (stamen) and female (ovary) reproductive organs on the same flower. (1) *Word origin for flower - 1150-1200; Middle English flour flower, best of anything < Old French flor, flour, flur < Latin flōr- (stem of flōs). Cf. blossom; Origin of stamen - 1640-50; Latin stāmen warp in upright loom, thread, filament, equivalent to stā (re) to stand + -men noun suffix; akin to Greek stḗmōn warp, Sanskrit sthāman place. Origin of ovary - 1650-60; < New Latin ōvārium. See ovum, -ary. (5)*

A petiole is a leaf stalk. On a compound leaf, the petiole extends from the stem to the first set of leaflets. A leaf without a petiole is sessile. (1) *Petiole word origin is 1745-55; < New Latin petiolus leafstalk, special use of Latin petiolus, scribal variant of peciolus, probably for *pediciolus, diminutive of pediculus pedicle. Stem origin is - before 900; Middle English; Old English stemn, stefn, equivalent to ste- (variant of sta-, base of standan to stand) + -mn- suffix; akin to German Stamm stem, tribe; see staff. Sessile origin is 1715-25; Latin sessilis fit for sitting on, low enough to sit on, dwarfish (said of plants), equivalent to sess (us) (past participle of sedēre to sit1) + -ilis —ile. (5)*

Phloem is plant tissue that conducts nutrients (food) through the plant. In woody-stemmed plants, the phloem is the inner layer of the bark. (Compare with xylem.) (1) *Word origin of phloem is German (1858), irregular; Greek phló (os) bark (variant of phloiós) + -ēma deverbal noun ending. (5)*

Photosynthesis is the process in which plants convert sunlight, water, and carbon dioxide into food (sugars and starches), oxygen and water. Chlorophyll or closely-related pigments (substances that color the plant) are essential to the photosynthetic process. (1) *Word origin for photosynthesis is 1895-1900; photo- + synthesis. Now your turn to look up photo and synthesis. (5)*

Pistillate flowers have a pistil or pistils. The pistil is the central set of female reproductive organs in a flower. The pistil is composed of one or more carpels and produces the ovule. (1) *Word origin is 1820-30; pistil + -ate. Pistil originated 1570-80; earlier pistillum, special use of Latin pistillum - pestle. (5)*

<u>Pollen</u> is the male reproductive cell of flowering <u>plants</u> and cone-bearing plants. Pollen <u>grains</u> are produced in the <u>anther</u> of a <u>flower</u>. (1) *Word origin for <u>pollen</u> is from 1515-25; New Latin, special use of Latin: fine flour, mill dust. <u>Anther</u> origin is 1825-35; New Latin Greek ánthēsis bloom, equivalent to anthē- (verbid stem of antheîn to bloom) + -sis —sis. (5)*

<u>Pubescent</u> means covered with short hairs or soft down. (1) *Word origin is Latin from 1640-50. (5)*

<u>Sapling</u> is a small tree between 0.4 and 5.0 <u>inches</u> in <u>diameter at breast height</u>. (4) *Word origin is 1375-1425; late Middle English; see sap, -ling. Another to investigate. (5)*

<u>Staminate </u>flowers are the male reproductive parts of a <u>flower</u>. It consists of the <u>filament</u> and the <u>anther</u>, which produces <u>pollen</u>. (1) *Word origin is 19th C from Latin stāminātus consisting of threads. Word origin for <u>filament</u> is 1585-95; New Latin filāmentum, equivalent to Late Latin fīlā (re) to wind thread, spin (see file) + Latin -mentum —ment. (5)*

The <u>tap root</u> is the main <u>root</u> of some plants often extending straight down under the plant with very little side branches (1) *Word origin is before 1150; (noun) Middle English; late Old English rōt , Old Norse rōt; akin to Old English wyrt 'plant', wort, German Wurzel, Latin rādīx (see radix), Greek rhíza (see rhizome); (v.) Middle English roten, rooten, derivative of the noun. (5)*

<u>Tawny</u> is a shade of brown tinged with yellow; dull yellowish brown. (1) *Origin is from 1350-1400; Middle English tauny; Anglo-French taune; Middle French tané. (5)*

<u>Tree rings</u> are used to determine the age of the tree. They are concentric circles that appear on tree trunk cross-sections that mark the end of a growing season. These rings show whether the tree grew a lot or a little that year. Each ring is made up of an earlywood and latewood layer. Also called annual rings or growth rings. *Origin is from 1915-20. (5)*

The <u>trunk</u> of a tree is the stem that supports the crown. Sometimes called the bole. (1) *Word origin is from 1400-50; late Middle English trunke, Latin truncus stem, trunk, stump, noun use of truncus lopped. (5)*

A <u>whip</u> is a slender, young tree consisting of a central stem with few or no side branches, perhaps 1.0m (3 ft) tall. (7)

<u>Wood</u> is the secondary <u>xylem</u> of <u>gymnosperms</u> and <u>dicots</u>, but the term wood is often applied to other xylem. Wood is used to make furniture, build houses, and make paper. (1) *Word origin is before 900; Middle English; Old English wudu, earlier widu; cognate with Old Norse vithr, Old High German witu, Old Irish fid. (5)*

<u>Xylem</u> (pronounced ZIE-lem) is a tissue in plant <u>stems</u> and <u>roots</u>. Xylem transports water and minerals upwards from the roots to the stem, via <u>capillary action</u>. Xylem is

strong and also provides support to the plant. The woody part of the tree. (Compare with phloem.) (1) *Word origin is from 1870-75; German, equivalent to Greek xýl (on) wood – ēma (5)*

References

(1) http://www.enchantedlearning.com/subjects/plants/glossary/index.shtml

(2) American Heritage® Dictionary of the English Language, Fifth Edition. Copyright © 2011 by Houghton Mifflin Harcourt Publishing Company. Published by Houghton Mifflin Harcourt Publishing Company. All rights reserved.

(3) Collins English Dictionary – Complete and Unabridged © HarperCollins Publishers 1991, 1994, 1998, 2000, 2003

(4) http://www.biology-online.org/dictionary

(5) All word origins are from Collins English Dictionary - Complete & Unabridged 2012 Digital Edition © William Collins Sons & Co. Ltd. 1979, 1986 © HarperCollins Publishers 1998, 2000, 2003, 2005, 2006, 2007, 2009, 2012

(6) http://www.saylorplants.com/ - Michigan State University

(7) http://www.treeterms.co.uk/